Being Christian
in the Twenty-First Century

You are Holding a Gift

From

Eldering Ministries

Being Christian
in the Twenty-First Century

Sam Gould

Foreword by Robert H. King

Foreword by Rodney Noel Saunders

WIPF & STOCK · Eugene, Oregon

BEING CHRISTIAN IN THE TWENTY-FIRST CENTURY

Wipf & Stock
An Imprint of Wipf and Stock Publishers
199 W. 8th Ave., Suite 3
Eugene, OR 97401

www.wipfandstock.com

PAPERBACK ISBN: 978-1-5326-1969-4
HARDCOVER ISBN: 978-1-4982-4619-4
EBOOK ISBN: 978-1-4982-4618-7

Manufactured in the U.S.A.   JUNE 13, 2017

All biblical quotations are taken from the *New Revised Standard Version Bible*, copyright © 1989, by the Division of Christian Education of the National Council of the Churches of Christ in the United States of America.

For our eight grandchildren,

Marissa
Timothy
Grace
Travis
Nicholas
Tyler
Emily
&
Katelyn,

who will face their adult journey in the twenty-first century.

The aim of the church is not to enlist its laymen in its services; the aim of the church is to put laymen as theological competents in the service of the world!

CARLYLE MARNEY, *PRIESTS TO EACH OTHER*

Contents

Study Guide

Foreword

CHRISTIANS ARE CHALLENGED TODAY as never before to examine their faith in order to make it their own.

Being Christian in the Twenty-First Century is an engaging, down to earth exploration of the meaning of Christian faith by someone grounded in the traditional teachings of the church, but viewed from a critical, present day perspective.

Sam Gould's background is business education and his questions are those of someone with a practical point of view, yet he is knowledgeable about current biblical and theological scholarship and skillful at relating what he has learned to the concerns of ordinary folks. This book grows out of his extensive experience teaching discussion classes for thoughtful, inquiring adults in a variety of denominational settings. It is not at all dogmatic and should provide a useful spring board for lively discussion.

For anyone seeking a contemporary understanding of Christian belief, I heartily recommend it.

Robert H. King, PhD
Dean Emeritus
Millsaps College

Foreword

HOW MANY LAY PEOPLE and clergy have serious concerns about the continuing decline in the numbers of people participating in Christian churches? How many of those think that decline is mostly or partly because of the church's refusal to consider newer and different biblical and theological perspectives that are relevant to the twenty-first century, most especially because of the daily increase in the acceptance and use of science and technology? How much will the lack of interest and involvement in the church from the strong majority of millennials, the largest generation ever born in the US, affect the future life and vitality of the church? How long will the church believe and think that it can keep doing what it has always done, but somehow get different results? Is it possible God is seeking to have people in the church consider some exciting and new and different ways? What if there was a book that helped Sunday School or other adult classes begin to consider and discuss these and other such questions, which could lead to dialogue that could help the church make needed changes? What if it was this book you are now holding and reading?

Sam Gould is a layperson who has thought a great deal about these questions, because he cares deeply about how the church is and isn't relating to the realities of the twenty-first century. His book is specifically designed to help laypersons and clergy begin to not only ask these essential questions, but also discuss them in ways that could enable and empower the changes essential for the future life and vitality of the church. He brings a college professor's ability, intelligence, and inquisitiveness to this book. You will be so very glad that you have purchased this book and started a faith journey of essential significance toward the development of ideas and actions that can help change the future of the church. May you not only enjoy the journey, but also the meaningful, enabling learnings that you experience.

Rodney Noel Saunders
United Methodist Pastor, Retired

Preface

*Happy is the person who meditates on wisdom and reasons intelligently,
who reflects in his heart on her ways and ponders her secrets.*

SIR 14:20-21

CHRISTIANITY IS UBIQUITOUS IN the United States and in other pockets of the world. It comes in many sizes, flavors, packages, and intensities. This is not the case in much of Europe where Cathedrals built for the masses remain largely vacant during Sunday services. In the United States many people are brought up in a faith culture and remain in it throughout their lives. But others find the religion of their childhood no longer suitable or compatible with their life experiences and fundamental world view. And so, people are leaving the church at a rapid pace. Are we as a nation following Europe's lead and turning away from our Christian roots?

In May of 2015 the Pew Foundation released a report chronicling the decline in Christian affiliation in the United States.[1] The report indicates that between 2007 and 2014 the Christian share of the population declined from 78.4 percent to 70.6 percent. Further, those who identify as unaffiliated, have grown from 16.1 percent to 22.8 percent of the population—an increase of nearly 42 percent in just seven years. Even many of the expanding nondenominational evangelical congregations are failing to keep pace with population growth. In absolute numbers Mainline Protestant and Catholic denominations have declined 12.2 percent and 6.3 percent, respectively,

---

1. "America's Changing Religious Landscape," 3-4.

over this reporting period. Faced with these daunting statistics one must ask, "Is there something wrong with the church?"

Perhaps one should ask if church affiliation is destined to be a relic of the past. Perhaps the church has served a purpose, but outlived its usefulness. Over the centuries the church has attended to the needs of the poor, the sick, and the uneducated. They have provided relief for orphans and widows. They have built hospitals, schools, and universities. But many of these functions have been taken over by local, state, and federal governments. Many of the fine colleges and universities with religious origins have since separated themselves from their founding bodies. With secular governing bodies now fulfilling many of these societal roles what is the church's role? Is it to focus on personal salvation while perpetuating the existing culture? Is it to give us space, perhaps an hour each week, to enter into a simpler time? Is it to entertain and make us feel good? If these are the case then perhaps the church has outlived its usefulness.

Many Christians uncritically accept church teaching and do not try to reconcile them with their experience outside of their religious life. That works just fine for many people. Yet, for many others their fundamental religious beliefs must coincide with how they understand the world works. For those people, among whom I count myself, there must be both head and heart. For these people, faith is most robust when the thought process behind it is sound and credible. Yet for many, ancient church dogma, doctrine, and creeds leave them incredulous. Perhaps it is the time for reform and renewal in the church. I personally believe that the church has an important ethical, empowering, and healing role to play in the twenty-first century. But, in order to do so it needs to focus on the character of its message. That means it must be intellectually satisfying as well as a place of comfort, fellowship, and service, a place where empathy and compassion are acted out consistent with the teachings of Jesus.

I wrote *Being Christian in the Twenty-First Century* for people who yearn for a deeper and more intellectually fulfilling understanding of Christianity. It is for those who have found adult Sunday school classes naïve and unsatisfactory, and worship services overly simplistic. It is written for people who want to move beyond a theology of sin, guilt, and wretchedness to one of uplifting love and empowerment. It is for those who no longer (or never did) believe that Jesus died for their sins, or that a supernatural deity controls everything and causes pain and calamity for some reason beyond human comprehension. It is written for people who wish to focus on salvation in this life, rather than an afterlife. It is for people who want to believe, but need help with their unbelief. It is written for those with the dilemma of not knowing what to believe when traditional church teachings are no longer plausible for them. If you fit into any or all of these categories, this book is for you. It is written to bring context to the way and how our faith traditions developed and puts into perspective the meaning of Scripture and doctrine for our time.

Sam Gould
Divide, Colorado, and Santa Fe, New Mexico
May 2017

Acknowledgments

No work is the sole product of one individual. Therefore, I must recognize those who have helped me along the path of discovery. That would include my wife, Elaine, who has not only been my soulmate for over half a century, but also an encourager and stalwart supporter. She has been my most loyal supporter and critic, bringing insight and relevancy to my life and work. I thank Dan Nicholson, for his down-to-earth critique of the early draft chapters of this book. Dan was the first to make many comments on the anticipated interest level and readability of the text as well as how I expressed key ideas. I thank the members of the Contemporary Christian Roundtable study group at Mountain View United Methodist Church in Woodland Park, Colorado. Discussion around several chapters led to similar refinements in the text. The Reverend Rodney Saunders, a retired Methodist pastor, made many vital contributions. Rodney introduced me to Walter Wink's thesis on Jesus as the "fully human one." He also introduced me to the sermons and writings of Carlyle Marne. Dr. Robert King encouraged me to go deeper in my contextual analysis and especially to trace the various atonement theories back to their cultic origins. Two pastors in my life standout as having influenced and affected me deeply. The first is the late Rev. Walter Fitton who showed Elaine and me the meaning of love and discipleship in the early years of our marriage. It was under Walter's mentorship and nurturing that I began my love of theology and program of study. The second is the late Rev. William (Bill) Youngkin. Bill was a true friend and man who lived his faith every moment. His commitment to living out the Gospel is a model that I try to emulate. I wish to thank all the educators who worked with me over the years to share their knowledge and wisdom and helped to form the person I have become. Finally, I wish to thank Brian Palmer, Matt Wimer, Chelsea Lobey, and Jana Wipf of Wipf and Stock Publishers for their professionalism that made the journey from manuscript submission to final publication a seamless process and enjoyable experience.

1

Being Christian

Some people keep silent because they have nothing to say,
while others keep silent because they know when to speak.

SIR 20:6

I AM WRITING THIS book from the perspective of a layperson concerned
with the future of the church. As we have all witnessed, church membership
has been declining over the past several decades with even the moderately
growing nondenominational evangelical churches failing to keep pace with
population growth. Part of the problem is undoubtedly the predominate
rationalism of our time and the undergirding propositions advanced by the
louder voices of evangelical conservativism, which many find unbelievable
and unsatisfactory as a basis for a faith structure let alone a worldview.

If you are a person that accepts doctrines such as the virgin birth,
substitutionary atonement, and bodily resurrection as literally true, then
good for you. This book is not for you. Please read no further. But if you
have given up on these notions and others as archaic expressions of the
Christian faith, or if you have put these notions in the back of your mind
and they only create dissonance for you on occasion, or if you are looking
at an alternative way of being a Christian and can stand the accusations by
some that you are not, then I urge you read further.

As a bit of personal history, I was baptized (sprinkled) a Lutheran
(ELCA) and as a teen I attended a United Methodist Church, mainly because my high school sweetheart did. It worked out well, we have been

married now for over a half century and she is still my sweetheart. After our marriage we lived in several different communities across the Midwestern, Southern, and Western United States. In each community we searched for a church in which we felt both accepted and challenged. As a result we have been members of Methodist, Presbyterian, Southern Baptist, and United Church of Christ congregations. During our short tenure as Southern Baptist we had to be rebaptized, this time with full immersion. I have served in about every lay leadership position these denominations have to offer. Additionally, I worked for twenty years in a major Catholic university as a senior academic administrator. In other words, I have been "around the block" in Christianity. But additionally, I have studied theology on my own for over forty years. My confession is that I have grown weary of the conservative Christian message which spoke to me once, but which no longer does. For that reason, my study has been broad over these past decades but has found a home in Progressive Christianity.

I am very fortunate to have been blessed with an ability for independent learning and an aptitude for teaching others. These skills have been refined and honed through the disciplines of advanced graduate work and endless practice, both artifacts of my professional life. But I have been even more blessed by clergy who have inspired and nurtured me over the years and by fellow travelers and seekers that have sustained me in my faith journey. But, that's enough about me. Let us return to the subject at hand. And that is, what does it take to be a Christian? What does being Christian mean, especially what does it or can it mean today, in the twenty-first century?

For starters, being Christian must entail more than subscribing to a static system of doctrines or beliefs. The Catholic theologian Hans Küng has written that Christian faith is simultaneously an act of knowing, feeling, and willing.[1] Being Christian is not limited to a belief system, but is an action that flows from one's beliefs that has a depth of knowing, and entails a proactive lifestyle along with the emotions that accompany it.

Knowing and believing are words often used interchangeably. But there is a distinct difference between them. Belief carries with it a degree of uncertainty while knowing encompasses certainty. But, can we really know anything? In the first century it was believed that demons caused illness. It was not until the late nineteenth century that the medical community understood that germs were a cause for illness and infection. From our infancy to our ongoing adulthood we learn new things that replace

1. Küng, *On Being a Christian*, 162.

old beliefs and understandings. As we grow and time unfolds around us, both individually and collectively, we learn through experience. We learn what is true, what works and what doesn't work, as we experiment and plow forward with informed trial and error. It is experience that gives us certainty and where we lack experience we must fall back on beliefs and their associated uncertainties. Experience gives us assurance.

So, what kind of things have a depth of knowing? Is it the doctrinal statements of orthodox Christianity? Is it creeds and dogma? And then a crucial question, "Does a failure to subscribe to these beliefs that in many ways defy experience disqualify one from being a Christian?" Or is there a more basic understanding of Christianity, a knowing that is appropriate for twenty-first century followers to which they can subscribe and be fully accepted as Christians?

Some have argued that the reason for the church's decline is that progressives have entered the picture and watered down the faith doctrines. They might argue that under progressivism one can believe almost anything and therefore people are choosing to believe nothing. They argue that we must redouble our efforts and increase our fervor for church dogma. But this is not the 1960s or even the 1990s. As Albert Einstein allegedly said, "The definition of insanity is doing the same thing over and over again, but expecting different results." Religion author, Phyllis Tickle, has written that Christianity reforms itself every five hundred years and that we are now due another reformation. Further, as theologian and author, John Philip Newell, has written, "Much of what is happening within the four walls of our household—liturgically, theologically, spirituality—is irrelevant to the great journey of the earth and of humanity's most pressing struggles."[2] Perhaps what is needed is a rethinking of Christianity, a new understanding of the how and why Christianity formed and its relevance in a twenty-first-century postmodern world."

For years, the voice of the liberal laity has been timid and louder conservative voices have predominated. Part of the reason for this is that conservative voices have their ready-made elevator speeches, i.e., simplistic reductions of complex thoughts into short messages that can be conveyed while riding on an elevator. It is these one-dimensional one-liners that condense and do violence to the beauty of the Christian message. You know what they are. "Turn away from sin." "Repent and be saved." "Jesus died for your sins." "Jesus saves." And there are more. In my small town a group with

2. Newell, *Rebirthing of God*, xii.

evangelical fervor can often be found shouting these pithy statements from a street corner at passing motorists. But it is time. It is time for those who have something more to say, to say it. The wisdom of Sir 20:6 quoted at the beginning of this chapter is appropriate. It is no longer acceptable, if it ever was, for those with more to say to remain silent.

This book reviews and comments on the work of numerous theologians, historians, sociologists, archaeologists, and biblical scholars, both contemporary and dating back decades and centuries. These scholars were and continue to be the prime movers for developing a new and deeper understanding of Christianity. With their help, in this book you should find more degrees of freedom in defining yourself as a Christian while at the same time appreciating truth wherever you may find it. You will be challenged to contemplate a different kind of world than the one in which we live. Hopefully your knowledge of "the way things are" and "the way they could be" will motivate a will to make things closer to "the way they should be." The integral unity of knowing, feeling, and willing will lead to a Christian faith that is life-giving and fulfilling.

Some of the religious controversies over the decades have spun out of misunderstandings of the context in which certain doctrines originated. Certainly, one of these is the doctrine of "justification by faith." What was Paul's intention when he wrote in Rom 3:28, "For we hold that a person is justified by faith apart from works prescribed by the law." Did he mean to contradict Jas 2:26 which says, "For just as the body without the spirit is dead, so faith without works is also dead." Were they actually talking about the same thing? What was the world like in the era that these statements were tendered? What does Paul's challenge mean for us today? These are the topics that will be addressed and discussed in chapter 2.

Chapter 3 is titled "Jesus: the Fully Human One." In it the life and times of Jesus are presented from a historical, political, familial, economic, public health, and religious perspective. Judaism's efforts to solidify their identity during this period are introduced. This background information is presented in more detail in Appendices I and II, for those who wish a more elaborate description. Jesus's likely socioeconomic status, education, and literacy are broached and his approach to Judaism that distinguished him from the prevalent Pharisaic teachings of the day are revealed.

In chapter 4 the topic proceeds from the pre-Easter Jesus to the post-Easter Christ. Here, with Jesus crucified, the story was supposed to end. There was to be no more annoyances from Jesus, no more followers, no more trouble for the Jewish aristocracy or the Roman overlords. But as we know, it was not the end. The scattered, weak, and bedraggled followers of Jesus regrouped and attempted to sort out what had happened. Who was this man? Was he the one Moses promised? Was he the messiah? Was he the *son of man* as describe in chapter 7 of Daniel? Perhaps even more importantly what do we think of this man today? Do we exalt him to a point where he becomes unfathomable, unfollowable, and unknowable? And as a result, do we, in the words of Howard Thurman, treat him as an object rather than a subject? Are some of the titles and thoughts we have about this post-Easter Jesus bathwater that should be discarded in a twenty-first century rethinking? If so, how is this done without throwing out Jesus? Further, is Christ God's rescue operation or as Paul Knitter suggests an opportunity for an awakening? And if the latter, what does this mean? The chapter ends with a mystical moment I experienced a few years ago, expressed poetically.

In chapter 5 atonement is addressed. What is atonement, what are its roots in the cultic practices of ancient Israel? What does the New Testament have to say about it? What have been the major concepts attached to atonement and how did the idea of penal substitutionary atonement come about? What are the assumptions about God, Scripture, and humanity that underlie substitutionary atonement and what are some other contours for an alternative understanding? These issues are addressed in this chapter.

Is Jesus the only way to God? This is the topic for chapter 6. The thought is from John 14:6 which reads, "Jesus said to him, 'I am the way, and the truth, and the life. No one comes to the Father except through me.'" Oh boy! This has caused so much trouble over the years. It is the basis for so much disparagement and even violence against non-Christians. God must cringe when this is uttered as it is so often in our churches. The task of this chapter is to delve into the Johannine community that wrote this Gospel. How did this community develop? What were their motives? How does John differ from the Synoptic Gospels? Should John be interpreted literally? What were the competing religious movements of this time? These are the issues addressed in chapter 6.

Chapter 7 is titled "Scripture: Word of God or Word of Man?" In this chapter, some of the conflicting understandings of God are addressed. For example how can God be compassionate and loving yet vindictive and cruel, ordering the genocide of whole towns and kingdoms? The concept of metaphor versus literalism is addressed and examples are given. Humor in the Scripture is demonstrated and examples of the incursion of culture taming or watering down Scripture are discussed. Finally, some suggestions as to how we should read and interpret Scripture are provided.

God is the subject of chapter 8. God is approached from Bonhoeffer's concept of the "great beyond in our midst." In this chapter, the origin of concepts of God stemming from an amalgamation of the chief Canaanite Gods in the pre-monarchical period of Israel is further discussed. Approaches to understanding God beyond anthropomorphism is advanced, followed by discussions of miracles and where we may find God. Tillich's approach of God dwelling deep within us is extended to plead for the unity of all beings and their responsibilities to one another.

"Church" is the title of the final chapter. In it is a discussion of things that must change if the church is to survive the twenty-first century. The issue of outdated doctrine is once more addressed, followed by a challenge to make the church again a critic of society as opposed to its collaborator. A case is made for the "immoral" church, i.e., a church that critiques contemporary morality through ethical analysis to reach higher levels of societal justice and compassion. This is followed by a discussion of timidity in the pulpit and a lack of curiosity in the pew. Congregations too often reach an agreement to avoid certain discussions that could deepen the understanding and commitment of Christians. A plea is made for Christian renewal through rethinking message, rethinking the church's role in society, and rethinking clergy/lay relationships. The chapter ends with Thich Nhat Hanh's observation that Buddha lives in his teachings,[3] and that likewise, it is precisely in Jesus's teaching that we find the living Christ. And thus, the plea is made to keep the resurrection of Jesus alive and bring truth and the seemingly insane sanity of God's wisdom back into the church and our lives in a thoughtful reformation and Christian renewal.

The preceding describes the purpose and outline of this book. If you are still with me, you should enjoy reading it and perhaps enter into discussions with others about it. To facilitate the latter, there is a study guide toward the end of the book. In the guide are instructions on how to develop and maintain an adult discussion group. Appropriate physical settings, administrative structure, the need for celebrating joys and supporting member's concerns, and rules for class behavior are fully outlined. The model is based on years of personal experience in establishing and leading these groups.

3. Hahn, *Peace of Mind*, 64.

The study guide also contains lesson plans for each of the book's chapters. Each lesson plan provides an outline that may be used to model each class. The outline contains an introduction to the topic, an opening prayer, sample questions to stimulate discussion, and a closing prayer. It is my hope that you truly enjoy and are enriched by this book. But, perhaps even more so, that you may find comfort and support being and growing as one of those questioning, doubting, and still learning twenty-first-century Christians. Welcome to the journey!

2

Justification by Faith

For we hold that a person is justified by faith
apart from works prescribed by the law.

(ROM 3:28)

IN ROM 3:28 PAUL wrote that "a person is justified by faith apart from works prescribe by the law." This statement has too often been set against Jas 2:17 which reads, "So faith by itself, if it has no works, is dead." So what is it that leads to justification or "being in tune" with God? Is it faith, or is it good works? Too often these two verses have been used out of context, distorting the meaning both Paul and James intended. This is the danger in taking verses out of context as "proof texts" to justify a particular action or viewpoint. Over the years this false argument has resulted in sharp divisions within Christianity as well as between Christians and non-Christians. The controversy for centuries has driven a wedge between Catholics and Protestants and justified adverse relations between Christians and Jews. The faith/works argument over time has morphed into whether one would be justified by doing good works or by believing the right things. This false dichotomy is not at all the argument Paul or James were making. This divisiveness flies in the face of Paul's understanding that faith should lead to unifying humanity and James's argument that one's faith should lead to charitable acts. Thus, we have two statements that when put into context are not in the least conflictual. That being set aside, in this chapter we will delve deeper into Paul's statement in light of what we have said about faith and with regard to the radical nature of his claims in the mid-first-century Greco-Roman world.

Before we begin, we need to make a disclaimer about Paul. Paul has been a very controversial person in the Scriptures for many reasons, a few of which will be noted shortly. Paul has taken a particularly hard hit from feminists based on statements attributed to him regarding women's roles in the church and their relationship to their husbands. Two particularly outstanding examples include the following. First Corinthians 14:34–35 reads, "Women should remain silent in the churches. They are not allowed to speak, but must be in submission, as the law says. If they want to inquire about something, they should ask their own husbands at home; for it is disgraceful for a woman to speak in the church." First Timothy 2:11–12 reads, "A woman should learn in quietness and full submission. I do not permit a woman to teach or to assume authority over a man; she must be quiet." These statements understandably do not sit well with many women today.

But was this really Paul writing these things? Marcus Borg and John Dominic Crossan describe the following distinct images of Paul depicted in Scripture:[1] a radical Paul, a reactionary Paul, and a conservative Paul. Bible scholars now believe that of the thirteen letters once attributed to Paul, seven were actually written by him (Romans, 1 Corinthians, 2 Corinthians, Galatians, 1 Thessalonians, Philippians, and Philemon). Three additional letters (Ephesians, 2 Thessalonians, and Colossians) are thought to be pseudo Pauline letters, i.e., written by contemporaries of Paul. The three pastoral letters, for many years attributed to Paul, are now thought to be written long after his death. They include 1 Timothy, 2 Timothy, and Titus. Borg and Crossan adeptly demonstrate a progression of radicalism being tamed to accommodate culture as one proceeds from Paul's genuine letters to the pseudo Pauline letters and finally to the pastoral letters. The one exception is 1 Cor 14:34–35 admonishing that women should keep silent in church and ask their husbands later if there is something they would like to have explained. These passages have marginalized women over the centuries, and sadly in far too many cases have denied them leadership roles in many churches. But there is a growing consensus that verses 34–35 were inserted into Paul's letter much later, long after his death. Clearly, Paul's authentic letters, including this one, attest to his recruitment of women to key leadership positions in the church. These women were frequently mentioned by

1. Borg and Crossan, *First Paul*, 13–15.

name. I can't imagine how they could fulfill such roles in silence! We will look at this and other radical views he had for his time later in this chapter.

Unlike Jesus, whose ministry predominately occurred in the sparsely populated Galilean hill country, Paul went to the major cities of the empire. For centuries, Jews had been relocating throughout the Roman Empire. Sometimes this was the result of forced displacement, other times it was by choice. In what has become called the Diaspora, Jews had built houses of worship or synagogues in the major cities around the Mediterranean. As Paul traveled to these cities preaching, teaching, and establishing churches, his first stop was often the synagogue. While built for the Jews, many Gentiles also attended them. Supposedly it was because they admired Jewish monotheism, morality, and family values which differed from the typical Greco-Roman cultural norms. In frequent cases they were also financial benefactors of the synagogues. These Gentiles were known as the God Fearers.[2] Before the fall of Jerusalem in 70 CE during the time of Paul's ministry, these God Fearers were prime targets for his message.

Paul faced many challenges. First, his message was not always well received at a synagogue. On five occasions his attempts at evangelism were reportedly met with forty lashes minus one (2 Cor 11:24). Secondly, the center of the new Christian/Jewish sect was in Jerusalem under the leadership of James, brother of Jesus. The Jerusalem crowd was skeptical of Paul's claim to be an apostle since Paul had never encountered Jesus during his lifetime. A disagreement arose between Paul and the Jerusalem leadership over whether or not Gentile converts needed to follow the Law of Moses found in the first five books of the Bible called the Torah, i.e., teachings or instructions. This body of instructions contained the Ten Commandments and a complex set of social, moral, ceremonial, sacrificial, purity, and dietary guidance for the Israelites that was believed to have been handed down to Moses by God. The Jewish practice of circumcision and prohibition of eating pork, shellfish, certain birds, etc. are some specific examples of guidance spelled out in the Torah. Both Paul and the Jerusalem group faithfully followed these practices. But for Paul, requiring Gentile converts to adhere to these practices not only created a substantial barrier to his recruitment efforts, but missed the point of his message. Paul in his letters to the Romans and Galatians makes his case that to be morally acceptable or justified before God one need not follow these practices, but rather live "in Christ Jesus." Stated differently, if one is committed to following

2. Stark, *Triumph of Christianity*, 80.

the teachings of Jesus they are justified in God's presence. Ultimately, Paul reluctantly swung Jerusalem Christians to his point of view, at least as recorded in his writing. Other scriptural and apocryphal accounts attest to ongoing differences between Paul and the Jerusalem leadership.

For a moment let us consider why Paul's message was so compelling in the ancient cities of the Roman Empire. The first century was a time of economic hardship due to Rome's heavy taxation levied on its vassal states. Its agricultural policies favored consolidation of agricultural lands. Many peasants, unable to meet the tax burden, were forced into bankruptcy and foreclosure, which facilitated the consolidation. This led to an influx of peasants into the cities. Added to this was the dismal lifespan of all but the elite of society. Death and disease were frequent and the average life of a peasant spanned thirty years. Family units were fragmented by poverty and early deaths. Rodney Stark provides the following description of Antioch, a city of 150,000, during the period. "At least half of the children died at birth or during infancy, and most of the children who lived lost one parent before reaching maturity. . . . A city with a constant stream of strangers . . . where crime flourished and streets were dangerous at night, where a resident could expect to be homeless from time to time."[3] Housing in the cities was dismal and construction shoddy. It would be centuries yet before the chimney was invented and homes, when heated, were poorly ventilated and smoky. One could imagine that many of these dispossessed and desperate people yearned for acceptance into a new social order to replace their splintered families. They were ripe for Paul's message of equality and caring for one another in community.

The agreement with the Jerusalem leadership cleared a major hurdle for Paul's attempts to attract Gentiles to his movement. With the requirements of circumcision and dietary restrictions set aside he was fully open for business. His argument that we cannot perfect ourselves through obedience to a set of externally imposed rules or rites prevailed. Instead, his message was that if people are willing, God will work in them, in spite of their imperfections, and empower them to set aside cultural differences and live as one in Christ. It is through this faith that one can be open to God working in them to accomplish this.

This begs the question, how are Küng's three components of faith discussed in the previous chapter, knowing, willing, and feeling, relevant to this discussion? For Jesus and Paul I think this was first a knowing that God

3. Stark, *Rise of Christianity*, 160–61.

is more than a clannish or tribal God. We are to understand and internalize the thought that all human beings are God's children. Our willful acts should be to love one another and to tear down the cultural, economic, and religious barriers that separate us and keep us from being the universal family of God. In this process our sense of compassion, selflessness, and unconditional love will ultimately reward us with feelings of worthiness, fulfillment, and the satisfaction of experiencing what it means to be fully human. That is the message of Jesus in his description of the kingdom of God as expressed in the Sermon on the Mount and actively practiced in his participation with folks from all cultural and social strata. It also leads us to Paul's proposition in Gal 3:28: "There is neither Jew nor Gentile, neither slave nor free, nor is there male and female, for you are all one in Christ Jesus." It is in subscribing to this principle and acting upon it that we become justified through faith and reap personal fulfilment.

Today it is hard to fathom just how radical Paul's statement that "all are one in Christ" was in his time. But consider the groups that Paul was working with and the deep divisions that existed and the barriers that he was working to tear down. For example, the Jew was forbidden to eat with the Gentile. While a Gentile would not find baptism an onerous initiation rite into Jewish-Christian fellowship, the Jewish practice of circumcision was a far different matter for adult male converts. Further, the Jew followed strict dietary practices unfamiliar and strange to the Gentile. In short, the Jew followed the law and the Gentiles did not. How do you reach a state of common love, compassion, and fellowship across these barriers? Paul fully recognized the differences yet said that "in Christ" we are all one loving community. The loving community is to be the overarching identity, not being a Jew or Gentile. Therefore, the law which differentiated these groups had to take a back seat.

Further, the gulf between a slave and a free person was deep and wide. Estimates run that as high as 80 percent of the populations in key Roman cities were slaves in the first century. Consider this description from Seneca[4] describing the gulf between slaves and free men that was written at about the time Paul wrote Galatians.

4. Lucius Annaeus Seneca, commonly known as Seneca, was a Roman Stoic philosopher, born in 4 BCE. In 65 CE the Roman emperor Nero condemned Seneca to death by suicide. Nero had the distinction of commanding the death of both the Apostle Paul and Seneca.

> The most arrogant of conventions has decreed that the master of the house be surrounded at his dinner by a crowd of slaves, who have to stand around while he eats more than he can hold. Loading an already distended belly in his monstrous greed until it proves incapable any longer of performing the function of a belly, at which point he expends more effort in vomiting everything up than he did on forcing it down. And all the time the poor slaves are forbidden to move their lips to speak, let alone eat. The slightest murmur is checked with a stick; not even accidental sounds like a cough, or a sneeze, or a hiccup are left off a beating. All night long they go on standing about, dumb and hungry, paying grievously for any interruption.[5]

There is neither slave nor free, for you are all one in Christ Jesus. This is a huge cultural shift for Romans to swallow. But it is the tearing down of walls between God's children that make one justified in God's presence. In other words, by expressing love and compassion to one another, God's presence in them becomes operable and apparent.

Finally, consider the phrase "there is neither male nor female." To say the wall between male and female was formidable in the first century would be quite an understatement. For example, consider the following: (1) *exposure*, the practice of abandoning female newborns in the forest to perish was legal, morally acceptable, and widely practiced by all social classes in the Greco-Roman world, and (2) even in large families rarely was there more than one daughter raised to maturity.[6] Consider the following letter excerpt written from man in Alexandria to his pregnant wife during the Roman era:

> I ask and beg you to take good care of our baby son, and as soon as I receive payment I shall send it up to you. If you are delivered of a child (before I come home), if it is a boy keep it, if a girl discard it.[7]

The male head of the family had the power of life and death over his household members, including the right to demand that his wife abort a child during pregnancy.[8] The instruments for abortion at the time were crude, as one could imagine, leading to subsequent disfigurement, infertility, and frequently death. The position of women in the Greco-Roman world

---

5. Seneca, *Letters*, 90–91.

6. Stark, *Rise of Christianity*, 97.

7. Ibid., 98.

8. Ibid., 120.

was further brought home to me a few years ago. I was touring the ancient city of Pompeii, which was preserved in volcanic ash for centuries and is now mostly exposed. This prominent Roman city's life ended in 79 CE, a little over a decade following Paul's execution. The openness of brothels in the town was evident and at intersections signs fashioned after a phallic symbol pointed the direction toward them for unfamiliar city visitors. The open sexual immorality was just one more instance of the humiliation and status of women in the empire. Lest one think that the status of women was only an issue in the Greco-Roman culture, and that the Jews had their act together with a more positive view of women, consider the following. In the Jewish wisdom literature promulgated for the faithful Diaspora Jews the following appears: "It is a disgrace to be the father of an undisciplined son and the birth of a daughter is a loss."[9] The birth of a daughter is a loss! Yet, in this milieu, Paul writes, "In Christ Jesus there is neither male nor female," a perspective he must have taken from the tone Jesus set with his own interactions with women. Again, this is a huge countercultural shift—a shift that was very appealing to women, especially those already with higher socioeconomic status in the Greco-Roman world.

In this first-century Greco-Roman world, Paul's message was radically countercultural as was the practice and teaching of Jesus who dined with outcasts and associated with the culturally acknowledged "low life" of his time. Being a full participant in the unified community of all of God's children is what it means to be "right" with or "justified" by God. Practicing a faith that encompasses a love for all humanity and that surpasses all cultural, economic, and religious differences is how one becomes reconciled or in tune with God. With the mind of Christ or as Paul writes "in Christ," we are a new loving, compassionate, justice-seeking creation living out God's vision for humanity. That is, we are justified, i.e., made right, by this active faith that includes, in Küng's terms, knowing, willing/acting, and feeling. I believe this is what Paul meant when he said that we are "justified by faith." Hence, there is no false dichotomy between faith and actions or supremacy of belief over acts. Action is an integral part of one's faith. And it is through these actions out of our will that we gain the experience that leads to knowing.

While we still have vestiges of Paul's world in that slavery still exists in places and differences still divide Jew and Gentile, male and female, these divisions are not as stark in the Western world today. We might ask, "If Paul

9. Sir 22:3.

was writing to us now, what groups might he include as having barriers that need to be torn down"? What groups need to reconcile their differences to live as one family of God's children? Would he write, "In Christ Jesus there is neither gay nor straight, neither Christian nor Muslim, neither sheltered nor homeless, neither rich nor poor, neither fundamentalist nor progressive, neither Republican nor Democrat; for we are all one in Christ Jesus"? Today, Christians, what walls do we need to tear down? Being one in Christ Jesus is still a challenge for all twenty-first-century Christians. But, it is how we can be justified by our faith.

3

Jesus: The Fully Human One

I came that they may have life, and have it abundantly.

JOHN 10:10

THIS MAY COME AS a shock to some, but Jesus Christ never existed. Jesus of Nazareth certainly did. He was a first-century Jewish mystic and prophet who had an understanding of the Hebrew God's vision for humanity that differed from the religious authorities and practices of his time. He drew upon the teachings of the Hebrew prophets and expanded upon them. So, just who was this Jesus of the first century? Before we can begin to answer that question it is important to understand, as best as our twenty-first-century minds can comprehend, the historical background and concurrent first-century conditions in which he lived and ministered. We will touch on many of these issues in this chapter, but for a more in-depth discussion please refer to Appendices I and II in this book. In this chapter we will discuss Jesus's response to the context or matrix into which he was born and lived. In chapter 4, we will address the meaning of Christ for the twenty-first century. The shift from Jesus to Christ is intentional. After his death and resurrection many of those who had known him believed he was truly the Hebrew Messiah and gave to him the title of Christ from the Greek word *Christos* which means *the anointed one.*[1] Jesus was given other titles as well. Son of God, son of man, prince of peace, and savior of

---

1. Anointing was the act of pouring a fragranced olive oil over an object or person to consecrate them or make them holy.

the world were just a few. Many of these were chosen to relate him back to earlier Jewish Scriptures, others to describe his uniqueness, and in still other cases to assert titles for Jesus that had originally been designated for Caesar. We don't know if Jesus actually referred to himself with these titles, and scholars have shed doubt that he did. However, his followers certainly applied these titles to him after his death.

In many respects the matrix into which Jesus was born and lived was much more complex than what has been thought and taught in our seminaries and church schools. Indeed, Galilee in the first century CE was in flux. It was still in the process of being resettled, new building projects had begun, a cautious Hellenization within a Judaic framework was in the process of becoming, and the region took pride in its new religious and national identity. Its economy was mixed, with differentiated wealth including a small middle class of manufacturers, business owners, and artisans. However, subsistence farmers and landless day laborers undoubtedly made up a substantial segment of the population. It was also a precariously dangerous time for anyone to challenge authority, either Roman or Jewish. We only need to reflect for a moment on the destruction of Sepphoris by the Romans in about 4 BCE or the beheading of John the Baptist by the Jewish tetrarch Herod Antipas to fully understand this. Into this matrix Jesus was born and grew into adulthood.

The traditional view of Jesus is that he was an illiterate peasant, imbued with the incarnation of God. Being God incarnate, he had no limits, except perhaps those that were self-imposed. But while focusing on the divinity of Jesus should give one cause to worship him or even fear him, it makes it difficult for one to identify with him, let alone emulate him. Perhaps it would be more beneficial to focus on the humanity of Jesus. Let's for a few moments pursue a less supernatural approach to understanding this man.

Traditionally it has been assumed that Jesus was a carpenter or son of a carpenter, meaning an impoverished landless dayworker. I am going to suggest that Jesus was not an impoverished, illiterate peasant. Rather, that he was probably the middle class son of a skilled worker, perhaps a master builder. Master builders were people with knowledge of how to build stone structures and were hired as consultants for those with wherewithal to pay them. But is this counter to the biblical witness? Not necessarily. Twice in the New Testament Jesus is associated with the carpenter's trade. Mark 6:3 says, "Is not this the carpenter . . . ?" and Matt 13:55 says, "Is this not the carpenter's son?" But the Greek word translated as carpenter is *tektōn*.

Tektōn had a broader meaning than what we today think of as a carpenter. It included carpenters, stonemasons, and builders, and there are more references to stone in the Scriptures by Jesus than to wood. Israeli archaeologist Mordechai Aviam has proposed a socioeconomic structure of first century Galilee that suggests that carpenters and stone masons were not at the bottom of the social structure, but rather between the lower rung and the upper rung, fulfilling a middle socioeconomic role.[2] Within the time of Antipas's building program such skills would undoubtedly be in demand. Furthermore, from a historical and sociological perspective, movements have not come out of the peasantry. One who spends the preponderance of their existence providing for the essentials of life do not have the time or energy to start movements as did Jesus.[3] Hence it is reasonable to assume that Jesus was not a member of the lowest socioeconomic class in first-century Galilee.

Nor is it likely that Jesus was illiterate and uneducated. His knowledge of Scripture is well documented in the New Testament and his reading skill attested to in Luke 4:16–17: "When he came to Nazareth, where he had been brought up, he went to the synagogue on the sabbath day, as was his custom. He stood up to read, and the scroll of the prophet Isaiah was given to him." Two predominate approaches to Jewish thought at the time were the Shammai and Hillel schools. The former advocated a strict interpretation of the Torah, while the latter was more focused on the overall welfare of the individual and took a less legalistic position with respect to the Torah. For example, the Shammai followers would be likely to point out that it was forbidden to strip grain from their stalks on the Sabbath, while the Hillels might be more likely to say the Sabbath was made for man, not man for the Sabbath. Jesus's ministry and teaching seems to have fallen more under the influence and educational tutelage of the Hillel school of thought than that of Shammai.

Here we have a young Jesus prepared for ministry, literate, well educated, with some degree of financial resources and a following. Many of his followers were women caring for his needs according to Mark 15:42. Next followed two mystical experiences. The first was his baptism in which he experienced God's approval and received the Holy Spirit. The second occurred during his time in the wilderness as he worked out his approach to ministry. His understanding of God became not of a distant almighty

2. Aviam, "Socio-economical Hierarchy," 37.

3. Stark, *Triumph of Christianity*, 90–101.

figure, but rather as a compassionate, loving Abba, i.e., daddy. It was a God that had a vision for what humanity was intended to be, and could be. Jesus undertook the role of becoming fully human and through his life and teaching gave us the blueprint for doing the same. He called this blueprint the kingdom of God. The kingdom is the new wineskin into which the new wine of Jesus's teaching is poured.[4]

Historical Backdrop[5]

Why do your disciples break the tradition of the elders?
For they do not wash their hands before they eat.

MATT 15:2

At the time of Jesus's birth Galilee was still being resettled, a movement which began about a hundred years earlier. Prior to this it had laid dormant and virtually unpopulated since the Assyrian assault and subsequent depopulation in 732 BCE. The resettlement began once the Maccabeans established Israel as an independent nation around 160 BCE. While this did not last all that long before the Romans became in charge, it was a period that had some very significant happenings. For one, some Jewish scribes and sages formed a group known as the Pharisees—the separate ones. They were at first supporters of the Maccabean ruling hierarchy, but later fell out of favor with them and were persecuted. Many, it is believed, migrated to Galilee, along with retired soldiers and younger landless individuals seeking to make a life in the rich farm lands of Galilee. Still others migrated to Galilee to avoid the civil dispute, exploitation, and skirmishes with neighbors that materialized under the Maccabean rule.

But, perhaps more importantly, after centuries of being under the thumb of Assyrian, Babylonian, and then Greek domination, they were free at last. That freedom brought with it a movement to form a wholly pure Jewish identity. Archaeological evidence suggests that in this period significant changes in lifestyle occurred. Fine earthenware, artwork, and evidence of imported wines available in earlier periods became rare. These

---

4. "No one puts new wine into old wineskins; otherwise, the wine will burst the skins, and the wine is lost, and so are the skins; but one puts new wine into fresh wineskins," Mark 2:22.

5. A more extensive coverage of this topic can be found in Appendices I and II.

and other artifacts of Hellenistic influences, e.g., frescos with depictions of humans or animals even in the homes of the wealthy became extremely rare or nonexistent. Instead, plain earthenware came into use as did a simple Jerusalem lamp and stone eating and drinking vessels believed to be purer than clay vessels. Step down pools for purification bathing were evident in many homes and public places. The Jews of this period were defining and differentiating themselves through their possessions and practices.

The Pharisaic influence during the period was dominant. Their movement sought to bring practices of purity once reserved for Temple worship to the Jewish home. They promulgated the *tradition of the elders*, a set of specific rules developed perhaps as early as the Babylonian captivity which made the abstract requirements of the Torah specific. They also professed a theology which basically placed God in control of all events. The implication that followed was that if you suffered misfortune it was because you deserved it and God was punishing you for your sin. If you were wealthy or fortunate in some other way it was because God was rewarding you. But, we will discuss this and its implications in more detail later. This is the backdrop into which Jesus was born, grew into adulthood and in which he brought a much different understanding of God, individual responsibility, and communal life.

Politics

At that very hour some Pharisees came and said to him,
"Get away from here, for Herod wants to kill you."

LUKE 13:31

Galilee was perhaps the ideal place among the Jewish client states for Jesus to practice most of his ministry. It offered a bit more freedom and tolerance for independent thought than Judea. Roman troops and Gentiles in general were somewhat scarce throughout the region. Judaism flourished in practice and in the thinking of its citizens, mostly under the tutelage of the Pharisees. Yet, as in Luke 13:31 we see that as Jesus gained larger followings he was in danger of Herod Antipas's wrath and displeasure. Quite aware of Antipas's beheading of John the Baptist, Jesus would have had to keep vigilance during his missionary journeys though the towns and villages of Galilee. Capernaum was an ideal home base for Jesus. Located on the Sea of Galilee, it provided a safety valve for Jesus. If he felt threatened he could journey a short distance eastward by boat to the Decapolis, an area not under Antipas's rule.

It is often argued that Jesus's ministry was of a nonpolitical nature. Much of it has stemmed from the verse in John 18:36 where Jesus, when interrogated by Pilate, says, "My kingdom is not from this world." The problem with this interpretation is that religious practice in the first century was endemic in all dimensions of one's life. Jesus's teaching touched all facets of one's existence, as we will see as we proceed. What became evident and problematic was that Jesus disdained the cultural stratification of society and the initiatives of Antipas that resulted in many members of the Galilean society falling into debt and losing their independence and livelihoods. We would consider that as being pretty political in today's culture.

Further, as we have noted in his inaugural address in the synagogue at Nazareth he read from Isaiah and is reported in Luke 4:18–19 to have said, "The Spirit of the Lord is upon me, because he has anointed me to bring good news to the poor. He has sent me to proclaim release to the captives and recovery of sight to the blind, to let the oppressed go free to proclaim the year of the Lord's favor." While this may go over the heads of many of us, it would have not done so to first-century Galileans. Indeed, this was a direct reference to the year of Jubilee, which was to occur every fifty years. In the year of Jubilee all land was returned to its original owners, debts were forgiven, and the enslaved liberated. Bringing justice to the oppressed as Jesus suggested he was about would, to Herod and others who had a stake in the status quo of Roman hegemony, be evidence of political insurgence worthy of death.

But what was Jesus's political agenda? Marcus Borg and John Dominick Crossan contrast the approaches to peace promulgated by Imperial Rome versus that of Jesus.[6] The imperial Roman approach to peace follows these steps: (1) consult the gods, (2) invoke violence, (3) be victorious, and (4) experience peace. It is what Walter Wink has called the myth of redemptive violence. "It enshrines the belief that violence saves, that war brings peace, that might makes right. It is one of the oldest continuously told stories in the world."[7] But, as Borg and Crossan have said, a peace so obtained is not peace, but only a pause in the violence. The steps in the kingdom of God approach promulgated by Jesus were: (1) consult God, (2) nonviolently

6. Borg and Crossan, *First Paul*, 120–21.

7. Wink, *Powers that Be*, 42.

confront injustice, (3) achieve justice, and (4) experience peace. The reality is that peace without justice is no truly lasting peace. Nonviolent confrontation of injustice in a prevailing world of redemptive violence may be successful, but as we will see shortly, frequently entails bloodshed.

Family Politics

Do not think that I have come to bring peace to the earth; I have not come to bring peace, but a sword. For I have come to set a man against his father, and a daughter against her mother, and a daughter-in-law against her mother-in-law and one's foes will be members of one's own household.

MATT 10:35–36

Wow, strange words, especially after what we just said about peace. Clearly these words attributed to Jesus did not mean that he would brandish a sword lest the passage in Matt 26:52, "Put your sword back into its place; for all who take the sword will perish by the sword," would make no sense. Jesus's words here mean that while the world operates under Caesar's recipe for peace, even nonviolent confrontation will lead to bloodshed. Need we go any further than the examples of Martin Luther King Jr. and Bishop Oscar Romero to make this point? But that is not the objective of this section. It is rather that Jesus understood that the restraining politics of the family and clan restricted the evolution of humanity into the universal love of neighbor as oneself.

Jesus's realm of God was broader than the familial, clan, and tribal focus of his time. He understood the tyranny and dysfunction that the ubiquitous patriarchal, familial, and tribal social structure engendered. Reinhold Niebuhr two millennia later put it this way, "A narrow family loyalty is a more potent source of injustice than pure individual egoism, which, incidentally, probably never exists. The special loyalty which men give to their limited community is natural enough; but it is also the root of international anarchy."[8] In Mark 3:35 Jesus is said to have commented that his family consisted not just of his blood relatives, but "whoever does the will of God is my brother and sister and mother." This not only speaks to the ideal of spreading love among all of God's children. It also speaks to the practicality of expanding the unsustainable family and tribal-based economy in which death, disease, and disability led many into destitution. Hence, we

8. Niebuhr, *Interpretation of Christian Ethics*, 70.

have biblical story after story of Jesus reaching out beyond family, clan, and tribe to exhibit inclusivity unheard of in his time. In the kingdom of God, family and tribal politics no longer ruled the day.

The Economy

Do not store up for yourselves treasures on earth, where moth and rust consume and where thieves break in and steal; but store up for yourselves treasures in heaven, where neither moth nor rust consumes and where thieves do not break in and steal. For where your treasure is, there your heart will be also.

MATT 5:19–21

What we have learned in recent years is that the economy of first-century Galilee was much more complex than a reading of the Scriptures or other ancient sources has led us to believe. It is not that the Scriptures are false or that those early writers were trying to be misleading. They merely spoke from their own points of view. Further, when we add what we know from archaeological and sociological research we gain a broader perspective of the issues that Jesus was confronting. The Galilean economy was a mix of agriculture, construction, administration, manufacturing, and trade. Permanent markets were only to be found in the major cities of Sepphoris and Tiberius. In those cities an appointed official ensured that measures were standardized and appropriate procedures were followed, bringing needed order and structure to these markets. But the official also set prices which may have led to exploitation of the producers. However, this power of price setting is not absolute. If overplayed, manufacturers and agriculturalists would find other means of production or surviving and thus lower the supply of the underpriced goods, which introduced a countervailing power into the market.

We also know that there were many wealthy families in Sepphoris and Tiberius. Undoubtedly they were large land owners, high-level administrators, and members of the royal court. But even the homes of the wealthiest did not match the splendor of the Jerusalem mansions. Further, all the wealth was not concentrated in the two major cities. Wealthy families having large land holdings and owners of manufacturing enterprises lived in the towns and villages of Galilee as well. One indicator of differentiated wealth in the towns and villages is the dissimilar quality, design, and opulence in housing uncovered in Galilean archaeological excavations of the last few decades. Wealth was undoubtedly unevenly distributed in the population, with large numbers of Galileans still living near a subsistence level. But there were also grades of wealth above subsistence which we may think of as a middle status between the very richest and the very poorest.

As mentioned earlier, Professor Aviam has proposed a hierarchical social stratum for first-century Galilee. The lowest strata were the day workers, shepherds, and beggars. Harvard Professor Elisabeth Schüssler Fiorenza would likely add others to this lowest strata to include low-level tax collectors, prostitutes, pimps, fruit sellers, swineherders, garlic peddlers, bartenders, seamen, public announcers, servants, the crippled, and criminals. In short, all those who were so poorly paid that they became marginalized, desperate, and often abused—the scum of Palestinian society.[9] In other words, those who Jesus *invited to the table*. Perhaps slightly above them or at the same station were the potters, spinners, weavers, and simple farmers either working for others or owning their own small plot. The middle level consisted of business owners of the small workshops producing olive oil, flour, or woven goods, and the more skilled workers including blacksmiths, carpenters, and skilled stone workers. At the top of the social strata would be merchants, agricultural middlemen, families of the oligarchy, tax collectors, and officials in Antipas's government, including the military.[10] In this respect and to some degree this economic differentiation is not unlike a class structure we could find today.

Further, the prevailing theology of the day supplemented with selective passages from the wisdom literature was broadly promulgated by the Pharisees. The theology in its most simplistic form says you get what you deserve. In other words, if you are poor, you are just living out the life that God has allotted to you. On the other hand, if you have wealth, it is God's blessing for your goodness. And how do you achieve this blessing? Follow the purity laws and tradition of the elders as taught by the Pharisees. But is that the way to salvation? Jesus had a different idea. He taught about an unconditionally loving God he called Abba, not one of condition and judgment. He drew from the ancient prophets and early Mosaic Law of justice for all, including the unfortunates, bringing good news to the poor, release of the captives, and letting the oppressed go free. He challenged the injustice of the economic attitudes and practices of his day in which some barely subsisted while others accumulated great wealth.

9. Schüssler Fiorenza, *In Memory of Her*, 128.
10. Aviam, "Socio-economical Hierarchy," 37.

Jesus does not condemn the wealthy, but instead he draws upon different parts of the wisdom literature which are consistent with the admonitions of the prophets to protect the orphan, widow, alien, etc. Such would be the case of Prov 11:25, "A generous person will be enriched, and one who gives water will get water." And Prov 22:9 which says, "Those who are generous are blessed, for they share their bread with the poor." He therefore speaks to his Jewish followers in the traditions of the prophets and wisdom literature which take a different tack from the theology of the Pharisees. And therefore Jesus addresses not only the wealthy, but also all those who see wealth as God's blessing. He is in effect saying, "Don't let economics define your life and quest for salvation." Don't let it limit you and consume your energy. You will not find salvation there.

Health

When Jesus had come down from the mountain, great crowds followed him and there was a leper who came to him and knelt before him, saying, "Lord, if you choose, you can make me clean."

MATT 8:1–2

Health in the first century was a precarious matter. Not only were the lowlands ripe with malaria-carrying mosquitoes, but any scratch or cut could lead to a life-threatening infection and death. Expected life spans were short, perhaps thirty years, with many children dying before reaching adulthood. Women suffered proportionately greater with numerous postnatal infections following child birth. Death was a frequent visitor and multiple generation families were rare. While physical illness was around every corner, the extreme stresses of everyday survival for many at the subsistence level must have led to various mental illnesses among the population. In many cases the teachings of the Pharisees reinforced the notion that all of the woes that could befall a person were God's punishment for some misdeed, either actual or imaginary. The prevailing religious theology in many cases led to isolation of the infirm and economic devastation to the family.

So Jesus was a healer. Healers existed in Galilee at the time. It is difficult to know their precise success rate and whether the healing stories were apocryphal or real. But Jesus did more than work to heal the disease; he worked to heal the person's damaged sense of self and their perceived unworthiness in the eyes of others and presumably God. He reintegrated these people into a society that shunned and isolated them and made them productive family members again. The leper asked him, "Lord, if you choose, you can make me clean." He didn't say, "If you choose you can clear up my skin condition." He said, "If you choose you can make me clean." You can make me accepted again in society.

Religion

Then he called the crowd again and said to them, "Listen to me, all of you, and understand: there is nothing outside a person that by going in can defile, but the things that come out are what defile."

MARK 7:14–15

Galilee, like Judah, was in its second century of practicing its Jewish heritage. That Jewishness was reflected in its purification practices taught principally by the Pharisees. As indicated earlier, stone vessels were prevalent throughout Galilee, as for example noted in the water to wine episode (see John 2:6), as were hand-carved lamps from Jerusalem or their copies, and miqwaoths, i.e., step down pools, used for ritual purification. Imported luxury goods were scarce and images of humans or animals were missing from frescos or other ornate structures. Salvation was being sought by promulgating strict Jewish purity practices to individual Jewish households, many of which were only previously applicable to Temple worship. Such strict adherence to these as well as the expanded tradition of the elders would bring salvation to Israel. Or would it?

Jesus broke the rules. He stripped grain and ate on the Sabbath. He healed on the Sabbath. He and his disciples ate without washing their hands. Jesus hung out with sinners and dined with tax collectors. He touched the *unclean* or allowed them to touch him. But he did more than break the rules, he rewrote them. With his kingdom of God he turned the whole moral fiber of the first century on its head.

Then he began to speak, and taught them, saying:
"Blessed are the poor in spirit, for theirs is the kingdom of heaven.
Blessed are those who mourn, for they will be comforted.
Blessed are the meek, for they will inherit the earth.

Blessed are those who hunger and thirst for righteousness, for they will be filled.

Blessed are the merciful, for they will receive mercy.

Blessed are the pure in heart, for they will see God.

Blessed are the peacemakers, for they will be called children of God.

Blessed are those who are persecuted for righteousness' sake, for theirs is the kingdom of heaven.

Blessed are you when people revile you and persecute you and utter all kinds of evil against you falsely on my account. Rejoice and be glad, for your reward is great in heaven, for in the same way they persecuted the prophets who were before you."[11]

These are all qualities that have nothing to do with political power, socioeconomic status, or religiosity. They are not what comes from external practice, but rather are conditions of internalities. It is not what goes in that defiles, but it is what one is in their depth and how they act it out that defiles, or conversely cleanses. Then Jesus goes into a number of topics saying, "You have heard that it was said . . . ," "but I say to you . . . " In his rewriting the rules he addresses anger, adultery, divorce, retaliation, love of enemies, and many additional issues. But Jesus did not intend to form a new religion; rather, he sought to bring Judaism back to its true roots in the law and teaching of the prophets. He says in Matt 5:17, "Do not think that I have come to abolish the law or the prophets; I have come not to abolish but to fulfill." And Jesus sums it all up by reaching back to Deut 6:5 and Lev 19:18, and stating in Matt 22:37–40, "You shall love the Lord your God with all your heart, and with all your soul, and with all your mind. This is the greatest and first commandment. And a second is like it: You shall love your neighbor as yourself. On these two commandments hang all the law and the prophets."

Confronting the social norms of the day and confronting both religious and political authorities is too often a death wish. This is especially true if the confronter speaks an uncomfortable truth. What matters then? Is it speaking truth, or is it sustaining the status quo, even when the status quo is terribly wrong? We know how the story ends. As Caiaphas, who was high priest at the time said, "You do not understand that it is better for you to have one man die for the people than to have the whole nation destroyed."[12] And so, Jesus was sent to the cross.

11. Matt 5:2–12.

12. John 11:49–50.

Jesus: Fool and Failure or Mystic Visionary?

Clearly the myth of redemptive violence has, with a few exceptions, prevailed over the years. But what could the world be like if Jesus's theology actually prevailed? By his model, justice would be achieved by compassion overruling legalism. Laws would exist to guide society's behavior and protect the powerless. Compassion would overrule punitive justice. Prisons, rather than focusing on punishment, would focus on rehabilitation and successful reentry of inmates into society. Nations would reform their budgetary policies to de-emphasize military expenditures in favor of building schools and infrastructure to undergird the possibility and potential for all of God's children. Politicians would work toward building consensus and solving problems rather than fomenting fear, spreading misinformation, and misrepresenting opponents merely to remain in power. Investment would readily flow into research and development for earth-sustaining technologies and renewable forms of energy. Children would not live in poverty or have their future determined by the part of town or the family status into which they were born. Quality healthcare would be available for all people. Information would be truthful rather than manipulative. People would care for and develop themselves, but also ensure their neighbor had the same opportunity. Greed would become extinct.

Conventional wisdom tells us that this is mere utopian dreaming. We can't afford these things. We must be realistic. Not everyone will ever play by the same rules. When some sense weakness they immediately take advantage of it. If this is the case, then how do we reconcile our faith with our practices? How can we call Jesus the son of God, the incarnation of God's true nature and vision for humanity and the Christ if we don't follow his teaching of nonviolent confrontation and distributive justice? Was he a fool and a failure with his idea of the kingdom of God where all could live peacefully? Should we not take him seriously? Was he simply a mystic visionary divorced from reality? Is he irrelevant? Was he ever relevant? These are perhaps the questions Christians must ask themselves in this century. If the answer favors relevancy, then what are we to do?

So where does this all leave us? Clearly, the Bible is full of examples of God turning over the tables on conventional wisdom. Over and again in Scripture the powerful are humbled and the lowly are exalted. Some through the years have taken Jesus's message seriously. It has not always turned out well for them in terms of our conventional wisdom. In many cases it turned out just as it did for Jesus. He said it clearly in Mark 8:34b,

"If any want to become my followers, let them deny themselves and take up their cross and follow me." Was he a fool and a failure with his avocation of the kingdom of God? The life and teachings of Jesus have been thought of as foolishness by some, yet the very essence of authentic life by others. As we live in ways that do not promote the kingdom's coming we perish moment by moment. As we do promote it, we find true life, what might be called the "eternal life."

Jesus was not a fool or failure. Nor was he merely a mystic visionary divorced from reality. He did not withdraw from society, nor did he develop a false piety, nor did he become a Roman collaborator. Unlike some, who were actively rebellious, he came not as a bandit or thief, but in accordance with the Scripture at the start of this chapter; he came to restore life to the fullest. Jesus was a seer of God's vision for humanity and assumed the full humanity as God ultimately intends for all of us. We have not lived up to our potential and God's dream for us; we are the fools and failures. We have not yet evolved into the full humanity of Jesus. But we have the model, and each of us can begin the journey into a fuller and more complete humanity.

4

From Criminal to Christ

The light shines in the darkness, and the darkness has not overcome it.

JOHN 1:5

WITH THE DEATH OF Jesus the powers of Rome and the Temple authorities believed they had effectively dealt with the annoyance of Jesus and his followers. They had crucified the leader and the followers scattered. Only a small group of mostly women gathered at the cross. Jesus, while potentially disruptive, had been nonviolent. It was said that even with the agony of crucifixion he refused to express hatred for his enemies. There appeared to be no further threat. The cross had put an end to all previous brigands, rebels, and insurrectionists. And this movement would also soon fade into obscurity. Job well done! The Jesus problem solved.

Or was it over? As the Gospel of John 1:5 puts it, "The light shines in the darkness, and the darkness has not overcome it." Violence may attack the truth, it may slow its acceptance or even seem to reverse it for a while, but it cannot snuff it out. Jesus's followers experienced this truthfulness with extraordinary power. It was a power so profound that later it would be argued that God had raised Jesus from the dead to be an eternal presence. Saul, the avid persecutor of the new Christian followers did not believe that Jesus could be the Messiah, executed as he was as a common criminal. Such a scandal was beyond reason. But Saul's post-crucifixion experience of Christ's presence, while on a journey to Damascus to roust out Jesus's followers, led him to the conclusion that God had validated the life and message of Jesus. After that event Saul became Paul, the Apostle, committed to spreading the Gospel throughout the empire.

But what was Paul, and the early Christian communities faced with? What hurdle did crucifixion present to the early followers? Death by crucifixion was certainly commonplace in the ancient world, having been used by the Persians, Assyrians, and even the Greeks. However, it was such a heinous form of death that it was rarely written about in ancient literature. Further, its purpose was to deter criminal activity and was reserved for brigands, murders, traitors, and rebels. In Roman times it was meted out to slaves, military traitors, and the lower classes. Since it dealt with the outliers and criminal element of the Pax Romana, its use had considerable support among the populous.

The Horror of Crucifixion

If crucifixion's aim was to deter criminal activity, it was clearly capable of such. The horrendous suffering it entailed was meant to put fear into anyone contemplating rebellion, insurrection, or other criminal activity. Other forms of execution, being burned alive, decapitated, thrown to the beasts, or hanging by the neck, had the advantage of being a relatively quick procedure. But crucifixion entailed long, drawn out suffering. It was generally preceded by scourging followed by a public procession through the streets carrying a crossbeam. Then the subject was nailed upright to the crossbeam. Occasionally ropes were used for fastening one to the cross in place of nails. A small cross section between the legs kept one's body weight from tearing arms and legs free from the cross. Puncture wounds suffered from the earlier beating bled freely. Slowly fatigue and muscle weakness led to suffocation when one's diaphragm collapsed and breathing became impossible. All the time this was happening, the victim knew that their only hope for relief was death. To hasten death the victim's legs would be broken, weakening their support structure, bringing on suffocation.

Crucifixion brought shame and humiliation. The victim was subjected to naked exposure and public suffering. In all but the very fewest of cases the body would not receive a proper burial, but would be left on the cross for days to be devoured by birds of prey and wild dogs or be cast in a garbage heap with the same outcome. Of all the ancient graves that have been found in Judea and Galilee, there has been only one found of a person who had been crucified.[1] The devout Jew who suffered crucifixion also knew from Deut 21:23 that he was under God's curse. Thus, the crucified were deprived not only of their life, but also subjected to dying a slow anguishing public death, with no prospect for proper burial, and an ultimate outright rejection by God.

The Movement

Having been executed by crucifixion, the punishment primarily reserved for wayward slaves, criminals, and insurrectionists, the movement had some explaining to do to convince people that Jesus was the Messiah. Recall that crucifixion was not just favored by a bunch of elite power brokers. It was broadly supported in the brutal society of the time and considered an appropriate punishment for outcast troublemakers. The religious authorities in Jerusalem clearly did not just want Jesus out of the way. That could have been done in less brutal ways. They wanted him completely discredited, for which purpose crucifixion worked perfectly. Further, those invested in the status quo would have thought his troublemaking ideas, turning conventional wisdom on its ear, eating with the low life, touching lepers, elevating the lowly, was just the sort of thing that crucifixion was designed to discourage.

One rationale that could be used to justify Jesus's crucifixion was the suffering servant passages in Isa 52:13—53:12. Here the redeemer is pictured as an abused servant of all. While these passages appear as describing a personal redeemer, it has been thought that the reference was to Israel as a nation. Yet these passages over time were applied to Jesus. And out of it came a whole new theory of atonement. But that will be a subject for a later chapter. The movement, under Paul's tutelage, as we saw in the last chapter centered in the cities of the empire among the Diaspora Jews and Gentiles. Its strength was in building communities that met the needs of city inhabitants. It promoted a supportive lifestyle of mutual caring that was unique in the Greco-Roman culture and the movement became known as "The Way," meaning a way of living.

Until sometime in the 60s the center of the movement was in Jerusalem under leadership of James, the brother of Jesus. But events soon developed that shattered this center of Christian leadership. First was the

1. For in-depth discussions of crucifixion and burial rites in the first-century CE see Hengel, *Crucifixion*, chapter 4, or Crossan and Reed, *Excavating Jesus* 230–70.

assassination of James sometime in the 60s. This was followed by the Jewish rebellion and subsequent destruction of Jerusalem in 70 CE. With these events the center of Christian leadership, still very much a Jewish phenomenon, shifted to the Diaspora and cities of the empire. It was then that over time the movement took on an increasingly Gentile persona.

Early Christian sects had many questions and held many different perspectives about this man from Nazareth. Was he human? Did he merely appear to be human? Was he the Messiah the Jews were looking for and Moses had promised? Was he the "son of man" of Daniel 7 that would return and usher in a new age? Further, how could the fact that Jesus was crucified as a common criminal be reconciled to a populous that largely believed that the crucified got what they deserved? Or if you thought him God or even the son of God, how could he have died? God can't die; God is eternal and certainly his offspring must not be mortal. These and many other questions surfaced during the late first century and thereafter as Christians sought to define themselves and Jews reeled in a similar confusion after the loss of their religious center in 70 CE

While different groups argued over whether Jesus really suffered on the cross or just appeared to suffer, or whether he was a messenger of God or of the same substance as God, for Paul and others, it was the strongly felt presence of his spirit on the road to Damascus or to Emmaus, or where several gathered in his name that his advocates became convinced that God vindicated the message of Jesus by resurrecting him from the dead. Death was not the final blow. Jesus lived on. In John 4:24, Jesus says to a Samaritan woman, "God is spirit, and those who worship him must worship in spirit and truth." Likewise, we must experience Jesus as living in spirit and in truth. Whether one believes the resurrection was physical, spiritual, or metaphorical we know that the living spirit of Jesus was and has been over the centuries a powerful force that has led men and women to endure ridicule, physical torture, and even death in order to give expression to his teachings.

Since the resurrection is so crucial to the validation of the life and message of Jesus, how are we to interpret this act in the twenty-first century? We do not have an experience of a man dead for three days suddenly becoming alive again. The Jesus scholars Marcus Borg and John Dominic Crossan have argued that the resurrection was not physical, that indeed, had a camera been available at the time the event could not have been photographed or recorded as historical fact.[2] Was this all metaphor?

2. Borg and Crossan, *Last Week*, 191.

In chapter 6 we will at some length discuss the Gospel of John and how it differs from other accounts of the life of Jesus. One clear distinction we will make is the Gospel's use of metaphor and the folly of taking the Gospel literally. The Gospel of John does give us some insight into the matter of the resurrection, making it clear that the resurrection was not physical, but that it is real. For example, Jesus's presence was strongly felt in a gathering of his disciples shortly after the crucifixion. John 20:19 states, "When it was evening on that day, the first day of the week, and the doors of the house where the disciples had met were locked for fear of the Jews, Jesus came and stood among them and said, 'Peace be with you.'" Thomas was not among them and when the disciples told him they had seen the Lord, he refused to believe them. But John 20:26–27 continues, "A week later his disciples were again in the house, and Thomas was with them. Although the doors were shut, Jesus came and stood among them and said, 'Peace be with you.' Then he said to Thomas, 'Put your finger here; see my hands. Reach out your hand and put it into my side. Stop doubting and believe.'" The locked doors are the key to interpreting these verses. Physical bodies, resurrected or otherwise do not suddenly appear beyond locked doors. Like so many other examples in the Gospel of John this is intended to be read metaphorically. It is the spirit and truth of Jesus that is to be worshiped and there are times when one feels his presence as though he was in the room with us.

While the stories of resurrection may be metaphor or parable, it does not mean they are not true. The Oglala Sioux holy man Black Elk makes this point when speaking of his people's origin stories. He is reported to have said, "This they tell, and whether it happened so or not I do not know; but if you think about it, you can see that it is true."[3] That was Thomas's situation and as he thought about it he knew that it was true. As was so eloquently expressed in the opening verses of the Gospel of John, the message and life example of Jesus, his notion of the kingdom of God, was truly the divine logos, the Sophia, the wisdom and true nature of full humanness that is of the nature of God that was incarnate in Jesus of Nazareth. Perhaps it can be snuffed out from time to time, but God will resurrect it on into eternity. And so it is with Jesus, his essence and spirit can still be present among us and through it we can have the inspiration for living the truly human life, and through it we find our salvation. This is what inspired so many men and women over the centuries to follow Jesus, the Christ. Perhaps theologian Harvey Cox has said it best, "The truth of the Easter cycle is that

---

3. Neihardt, *Black Elk Speaks*, 4.

the life work of Jesus was not annihilated by his execution. It continues, among both those who follow him explicitly and those who contribute to the realization of the 'possible world' that he demonstrated, whether they acknowledge him or not."[4]

While a complete history of the early Christian movement's trials and tribulations is beyond the scope of this chapter, let it be said that the movement did gain momentum throughout the Roman Empire as people of conscience and goodwill incarnated the nature and spirit of the very much living Christ. But they were not all of the same cloth. There were disagreements as to how to understand the meaning Jesus. Attempts to constitute an orthodoxy and discern the true faith began as early as the appearance of the Pastoral Letters and the Epistles of John. As was inevitable, human nature developed factions to define right belief. Subsequently the letters of Paul, and the Gospels of Luke and John, took on increasing importance within the Christian communities. Further work was undertaken to codify Christianity, to develop a canon of legitimate writings that would be the basis for Christianity. During this period there were periodic episodes and pockets of persecution, but the movement continued and increasingly more individuals of rank and wealth joined the movement. As the numbers of Christians grew in the empire by the early fourth century it occurred to the emperor Constantine that Christianity could become an integrating factor within the empire. But to do so there had to be some undergirding and commonly acknowledged principles as to what Christianity was. In 325 CE Constantine convened a Council of Bishops at his palace at Nicaea and the foundation of Christian orthodoxy was established. It was now possible to identify the true Christian as different from a Jew as well as from other religious adherents. This caused an important and perhaps unanticipated change to occur in the Christian movement which now had the power of the empire backing it. The defining element of a Christian was no longer the way one lived, but rather what one believed. As it has been astutely pointed out there is no mention of what to believe about Jesus in the Sermon on the Mount and no mention of how to live in the Nicene Creed. The power of the empire now was the power behind the church. Overzealousness led to the branding of heretics whom for centuries were tortured and executed. This transformation of faith from a way of life into what one must believe has persisted in many Christian sectors for over 1,700 years, and is still alive and well in much of Christendom today. In the twenty-first century,

---

4. Cox, *Future of Faith*, 53.

with few exceptions, Christians have moved beyond torturing and killing one another over differences in beliefs. However, this focus on belief, especially those beliefs that are no longer tenable, is leading to a malaise among the congregants that can be heard as footsteps leaving the church. As the author and lecturer Brian McLaren has recently written, "What would it mean for Christians to rediscover their faith not as a problematic system of beliefs but as a just and generous way of life, rooted in contemplation, and expressed in compassion? Could Christians migrate from defining their faith as a system of beliefs to expressing it as a loving way of life?"[5] And so, how should we practice Christianity in the twenty-first century? What is our stance toward this Christ? Is Christ still relevant? Which beliefs should we hold on to and which should we jettison? These are the issues we discuss in the remainder of this chapter.

Religious Subject or Religious Object?

Howard Thurman was an African American author and civil rights activist who grew up in the segregated South in the early decades of the twentieth century. He served as the first dean of Rankin Chapel at Howard University. Later, for over a decade, he held the position of dean of the Marsh Chapel at Boston University and taught in Boston University's School of Theology. Thurman was an advocate for nonviolent civil disobedience as a strategy for cultural change. His most influential book, *Jesus and the Disinherited*, deeply influenced Dr. Martin Luther King Jr. and other civil rights leaders of the 1950s and thereafter. Thurman once described an insight he had after being asked to explain why he was a Christian. He said he felt challenged to write about Jesus as a *religious subject* rather than a *religious object*.[6]

What could Thurman have meant by this? As a subject, Jesus's teachings provide us with the road map as to how we are to live as Christians. But once we move to a post-Easter Christ narrative, Jesus becomes far beyond what any of us can aspire to emulate. The creeds have literally made him God incarnate, the equal of God, of the same substance as God, the second person in the Trinity. The emphasis on Christ does not lie in honoring Jesus's vision of God's goodness and taking it as direction for our lives. Rather, it lies in Jesus becoming an object that gives credence to our pleadings for God's mercy. When we end a prayer with "in Jesus's name we ask this," are

5. McLaren, *Great Spiritual Migration*, 2.
6. Thurman, *Jesus and the Disinherited*, 5.

we really thinking of Jesus pointing to the nature of God? Or are we using Jesus as a tool for getting God's attention? Thurman sought to study Jesus as subject and not, as so often happens, as an object for gaining God's favor.

Christ as an object places us in the position Whitehead has described as an early stage of religion.[7] That is, practicing and using religion to save ourselves. Hence salvation's meaning becomes not about internalizing the values of God revealed in Jesus's life and teachings, but about an external motivation of believing and perhaps acting in order to save ourselves from eternal damnation and/or ensure an eternal existence of postmortem bliss. This is a fear/guilt/compensation motivation for faith which so often becomes unsustainable.

Consider the following alternative. Let us move beyond what Borg and Crossan have called *heaven and hell* Christianity to Jesus as the subject of our faith; and, by doing so, experiencing the eternal life of truth and worthiness. Jesus sowed the seeds for a truly revolutionary way to live and love. Jesus's message is and remains revolutionary because not many of us have internalized it. John Yoder, the University of Notre Dame theologian and ethicist best known for his advocacy for Christian pacifism, entitled one of his books *The Original Revolution*. He did this for an obvious reason. It is because if we truly followed what Jesus proposed, we would not be the darlings of our social networks, but the gadflies of our culture and often even the revolutionaries of our time. By his life and teaching Jesus provided us with the possibility of an awakening to what it would mean to be fully human and aware of the ever-present loving God in whom "we live and move and have our being."[8]

This internalization and "awakening," as Paul Knitter[9] might phrase it, is what I think Thurman may have meant by Jesus as a religious subject. Christ then becomes more than a religious object to be venerated and worshipped on Sunday mornings. As subject, Christ lives in us as the eternal logos and truth, transforming and delivering us from total preoccupation with ourselves and opening us to the universal oneness of creation. This is being alive in Christ. This is truly salvation!

If we were to truly open ourselves to this salvation, what would it look like? That is the beauty of Jesus. Not only was he a teacher, but he also was the illustrator, the one who was perfectly unified. He lived as he taught.

7. As described in Cobb and Griffin, *Process Theology*, 43.

8. Acts 17:28.

9. Knitter, *Without Buddha*, 116–17.

His love so transcended fear and lack of sufficiency that Divinity radiated through him. He not only told us how to live, he showed us. His life example then is a fully evolved model of humanness for us to incorporate within ourselves should we submit to his salvation. This state of being fully human is what it means to be truly divine.

The kind of life Jesus led eschewed violence, but nevertheless engaged in persistent nonviolent confrontation of injustice in all of its societal forms, both individual and institutional. Unfortunately, this does not always end pleasantly. Just think of Jesus, Stephen, Peter, Paul, Justin Martyr, Origen, Tyndale, More, Gandhi, Evers, King, Romero, Rabin, Bhutto, Malala Yousafzai (almost), and whoever is next. Jesus says in Matt 10:38, "Whoever does not take up the cross and follow me is not worthy of me." This is not easy to follow and we must ask, "What does that mean for you and me?" What does it mean for us in the twenty-first century?

We are now well over a decade into a new millennium, nearly 2,000 years since Jesus showed us "the way." Have we forgotten or perhaps never understood the message? By the frequency of war and the pain of human suffering we certainly haven't internalized the message or if awakened, have not acted on it. Perhaps we have made some progress toward this understanding of God's vision for humanity. Deep in our consciousness we know this vision is right. But do we have the courage to double down on our efforts to move this agenda forward? Can we move beyond our fears and our self-interest to take up the life Jesus lived? If we did, how might that look in today's world, both for the individual and for society at large? These are the fundamental questions that Christians should ponder today.

Jesus and the Bathwater

With much of Christianity having evolved into a system of beliefs, are there some commonly held beliefs that should be jettisoned? Many progressive theologians and Bible scholars have called for a revision of orthodoxy. They have argued that Christianity is on the verge of extinction if significant change does not occur in the church and its teachings. They argue that indeed the twenty-first-century mind cannot much longer abide a faith that is anchored in antiquity. Recently I had lunch with a dear friend who teaches in a conservative evangelical seminary. In the course of our discussion we came to the conclusion that we both are concerned about the future of Christianity, but approach it from very different perspectives and assumptions. Our concern is that the church would continue to decline in the twenty-first century if some changes did not occur. For my friend, while I am sure that I will only abysmally represent his position, it was that the orthodox teachings of the church should be reinforced to provide the guardrails to keep the faith on course and true to tradition. For me it was placing many of the creeds and doctrines of the church in a basket to be set aside, go back to the basic teachings of Jesus as understood from a first-century perspective, and restate them in a twenty-first-century framework. All the time emphasizing the humanity of Jesus to which all of us can connect. The Catholic theologian Edward Schillebeeckx has expressed it this way: "The crisis in the church's use of language, in her creeds, liturgy, catechesis, and theology, therefore points to the fact that this language can no longer be experienced by many believers as a reflection of their contemporary association with reality."[10]

But if we follow this path of discarding creeds and doctrines, our challenge will be to identify the guardrails that will keep us within the Christian family as opposed to drifting into an undisciplined spirituality. In other words, how do we throw out the traditional teachings and doctrines of the church without throwing out Jesus? What in essence is the bathwater to be discarded and what is the baby worthy of keeping?

I believe the argument comes down to what is essential to establish the authority of Jesus as our window to the essence of God. By essence I mean the values and vision as to how we should live and relate to one another as expressed in Jesus's kingdom. Is the life as expressed in the teachings and living example of Jesus sufficient as verified by experience? In the instances where his teachings are followed, surely goodness and mercy flow. Often when it is ignored misery and devastation follow. Is this enough to establish Jesus's authority or do we need more? Do we need a miraculous birth? Do we need healing and feeding miracles? Do we need transfigurations on mountain tops and bodily resurrections? Or can we attribute all these assertions to an ancient writing style that slanted heavily toward metaphor and hyperbole? My friend might say, whether we need them or not is irrelevant and doesn't in the least indicate that they did not actually happen. If he did say this he would be absolutely correct. Our need does not deny or affirm if something in fact happened.

But we do have some evidence that everything written about Jesus could not have literally happened the way it was written. For example, when

10. Schillebeeckx, *Understanding of Faith*, 15.

did Jesus become the "son of God'? Paul would say at the resurrection (Rom 1:4); Mark would say at his baptism (Mark 1:11); Matthew and Luke would say at conception (Matt 1:18, Luke 1:35); and John would say he was the *logos* that existed from the beginning of time (John 1:1–14). Here we have several different interpretations that arose over a relatively short period of time. Paul is thought to have written prior to 64 CE, Mark 66–70 CE, Matthew and Luke 80–90 CE, and John's finished version 90–100 CE. This evolution of thought seemed to embellish the stature of Jesus from Paul to John over a period of about thirty-five years. One might argue that the most authoritative account would be the earliest, but that may not be the case. If revelation continues it may well be that later insights clarify truth rather than distort it. If that is the case then the door is open for revelation that continues even today and revision of the orthodoxy developed in the early fourth century is long overdue for update and revision. Indeed, given all we have learned in the intervening centuries, it not only calls for us to do this, but obligates us to do it.

Continuing revelation brings into play my friend's question, what are the guardrails that keep the "faith" on the road rather than flying off over the cliff? Is it the ancient creeds of tradition or is it the interpreted message of Jesus. Perhaps the ancient creeds can be reinterpreted in a metaphorical manner and placed in the context of the time of their authorship. But the stumbling block for many is how they were used to empower the hierarchical church and provide excuses for eliminating opposing views through the execution of heretics. Further, interpretation of the creeds in a way that may make sense for today takes considerable explanation which those unfamiliar with the church may find laborious if not nearly impossible to understand.

Therefore, I would stake my bet on a meaningful interpretation of the humanity and teachings of Jesus and their prerequisites in the Old Testament for sustaining Christianity in contemporary society. Intention, behavior, and lifestyle within these guidelines are the guardrails or criteria for living a Christian life. Further, the exclamation points provided by a literal interpretation of Scripture associating Jesus with a virgin birth, miraculous healings, feeding the multitudes, mountain transfigurations, bodily resurrection, and the like, may need to be a relic of the past. Let those who need these additional proofs abide with them. However, it might serve us well to realize that over the centuries a literal interpretation and adherence to creeds and doctrine have not been effective guardrails for the Christian life. Rather they have provided justification for much inhumane behavior at both the personal and societal levels. These propositions may well be the bathwater that needs discarding for many contemporary committed and "could be" Christians. Put simply, we do not need to engage in mind twisting that distorts Jesus's message of love with superfluous complexities and literal reading of mythical account.

Abandoning the bathwater and keeping the essence of Jesus's spirit alive would be a very positive step for preserving Christianity. Jesus, rather than being an object that we take out and dust off when we are in some sort of a pickle, should be the subject that keeps us in the guardrails of Christian thought and tradition. However, while we jettison the hyperbolic claims placed on Jesus after his death, we still have the Christ problem. How are we to interpret and experience this living Christ?

Theologian Paul Tillich wrote that we find the divine deep within ourselves. But that too many of us rush around on the surface of our lives, seldom if ever experiencing the divine. I believe we touch the Christ spirit when we grieve or face the possibility of tremendous loss. At those moments we feel most alone and reach for the divine. But should that be the only time we reach out? Dietrich Bonhoeffer, the martyred German theologian, wrote from prison that we should invite the divine into the center of our lives and not relegate it to the margins of life. That is, we should seek the Christ spirit in our everyday lives. Some of us experience the divine in scenes of beauty, or the sound of music, or in metaphorical poetry, or in the touch of a loved one. Awakening moments are typically fleeting, but they give one a sense of wonder and of the mystery of divinity that can bring transcendence of the soul to a realization of oneness and unity with all of creation. One such moment for me led to a poem I wrote to try to capture that moment. It appears at the end of this chapter.

The Christ experience is both transcending and empowering. In touch with it we grow beyond ourselves and see ourselves as part of a larger whole, interconnected with all beings. It is empowering in that it moves us to act in ways that do no harm, but seek to enrich all. Rather than a theology built on the premise of sinfulness and depravity, it builds on the hope that divinity can reside in us and us in it. While imperfect, I can be assured that the Christ spirit can work in me to make me better tomorrow than I am today. That is a life to look forward to, to enjoy and rejoice in. But the Christ spirit only comes when we make space for it. While our lives may require rushing around on the surface much of the time, we must intentionally take time to empty ourselves and make room for Christ to enter. Christ as spirit empowers us to transcend our self-preoccupation and dance with the divine to remain within the guardrails.

I and Thou:
You Danced for Me

We sat in the sunlight,
That early fall morning,
The tree and I,
Each in our separate worlds of being.

It was tall, but majestic and full,
Its leaves golden,
Not unlike others about it,
Reflecting the autumns of their lives.

A breeze began to excite her branches.
She then took leave of being an it,
Transcending ordinariness,
Blissfully becoming and fulfilling her destiny,
Of entering into relationship,
It was no longer a tree and me, but
You and I in solidarity.

Sensing my mood,
You began to dance for me.
Resisting morning breezes, then submitting,
Wavering never in simplistic unison, but
In a symphonic ebb and flow.
Movements so gracefully synchronous,
As though inspired by a Mozart sonata,
That only you could embody,
And I could imagine.

I sat in the sunlight now mesmerized,
Aware that you danced only for me.

God is in all of creation,
Playfully there to surprise and delight us.
Bringing us into relationship,
Making the ordinary extraordinary
As if turning pedestrian water into epicurean wine.

We can drink it,
If we take the time.

I sat in the sunlight that early fall morning, but
Now enriched and fulfilled,
Not as a tree and I, but rather,
In oneness with Creator and creation.

Sam Gould

5

Atonement

You shall bring to the priest a ram without blemish from the flock, or the equivalent, as a guilt offering; and the priest shall make atonement on your behalf for the error that you committed unintentionally, and you shall be forgiven.

LEV 5:18

WOW, ATONEMENT! WHAT IS it? Animal sacrifice seems so odd, primitive, and barbaric to the twenty-first-century mind. What is it all about? Probably the easiest explanation of atonement is that it is a method for gaining God's acceptance or perhaps forbearance. Some have broken the word down into at-one-ment, meaning most simply "being in sync with God" or being "one with God." The rituals for achieving atonement in ancient Israel are laid out in the Pentateuch, the first five books of the Bible also known as the Law. Both Exodus and Leviticus contain lengthy descriptions of how atonement is to be obtained.

Animal and grain sacrifice to the gods was endemic in the ancient world. Israel was not the originator of the sacrificial cult, rather they assumed it from the cultures from which they evolved. It was widely practiced by the Babylonians, Canaanites, Moabites, and others. Atonement meant appeasing God and obtaining purity or forgiveness for transgressions. The first instance of sacrifice in the Bible occurs in Gen 4:3–4 with the offerings of Cain and Abel. As we know, this first sacrifice did not work well for either Cain or Abel.

A crucial question is what is the nature of this god that the Pentateuch is addressing? Without some conception of this, it would make little sense to devise ways to stay on the good side of this god. Perhaps it is best said that it was a god of conditional compassion. Examples abound from being cast from the Garden in Gen 3, to the destruction of all creatures sans Noah, his human companions, and animal refugees, to Moses pleading for mercy from an angry god filled with wrath for the people in the desert having made the golden calf, and so on. As long as the people followed the commandments all was well, but cross over to the other side and all hell broke loose. Hence, this god's compassion was conditioned on the behavior of the people. But how could this god's wrath be tamed and the people restored to good graces after they had wandered into sinfulness? An obvious answer was to offer a gift to this god. It had to be something of high value to the transgressors else it would not seem a sincere repentance.

In the ancient mind-set of a three-tiered universe with their god residing above in Heaven, one way to reach god would be through a burnt offering. A burnt offering would provide pleasing aromas wafting up to the heavens. This apparently was the notion that Noah had once he reached dry land. Genesis 8:20–22 recounts how the Pentateuch's god can be mellowed by the pleasing odor of burnt offerings, promising never again to destroy every living creature. The cult of sacrifice believed they could appease or mellow this conditionally compassionate god with the aromatic smells emanating from the meeting tent and later the Temple altars. Of course, to express true repentance, a suitable sacrificial animal must be unblemished, the best and most valuable of the herd or flock. In some ancient cultures, including at times Israel, the most valued sacrifice was a first born son, i.e., a human child. However, the episode of Abraham and Isaac in Gen 22 put an end to this practice at least as a sanctioned cultic event. As the Abraham/ Isaac story indicates, the blood of the ram was a sufficient substitute for the blood of Isaac.

During the post-exilic desert experience described in the Old Testament, blood was considered the life force of all creatures and was believed to be a purifier. The blood from sacrifices was used to purify the altar, the container for the Mercy Seat covering the Ark of the Covenant, and priestly vestments. It was even used in a ceremony to consecrate priests by dabbing it on their ear lobe, finger, and toe. The sins of the Israelite community were believed to physically defile the altar and Mercy Seat, which were purified by sprinkling blood on them. As stated by Professor Stephen Finlan, the sprinkling of blood acted as a spiritual detergent to purify these holy items.[1]

---

1. Finlan, *Problems with Atonement*, 13.

On the Day of Atonement, an annual event, the scapegoating ritual was undertaken. Two unblemished goats were brought forth. Lots were cast to determine God's preference. One goat became a burnt offering. The other was chosen to lay upon it all the sins of the community for the past year. It was then abandoned, sometimes thrown over a cliff, and then driven into the desert to perish. Thus, the sins of the community were transferred from the community onto the scapegoat and it became a substitute recipient for God's wrath and sent to perish under the power of the demons of the desert.

Atonement was also achieved through the half shekel of the sanctuary tax. All Israelites twenty years and older were obligated to annually give one half shekel to the maintenance of the priesthood and sanctuary as commanded in Exod 30:12–15. It reads,

> When you take a census of the Israelites to register them, at registration all of them shall give a ransom for their lives to the LORD, so that no plague may come upon them for being registered. This is what each one who is registered shall give: half a shekel according to the shekel of the sanctuary (the shekel is twenty gerahs), half a shekel as an offering to the LORD. Each one who is registered, from twenty years old and upward, shall give the LORD's offering. The rich shall not give more, and the poor shall not give less than the half shekel, when you bring this offering to the LORD to make atonement for your lives.

To recap, the ancient practice of atonement entailed several aspects. First was an effort to appease the easily aroused wrath of their god through aromatic smells of an unblemished sacrifice. Second, was to achieve purification though the sacrifice ritual with blood as the spiritual cleanser. Third, was to transfer the sins of the community onto an unsuspecting goat that was sent into the wilderness. Fourth, was to purchase or pay a ransom that would atone for one's sins. These were all common ways of pleasing gods and purchasing salvation in the ancient world. These methods of atoning were familiar to Israelites and Gentiles alike.

Making Sense of the Crucifixion

As we discussed in the previous chapter, there was some explaining to do. Jesus, was crucified as a common criminal and insurrectionist. If Jesus was the anointed one how could he have been crucified? How can the argument that Jesus was the Messiah be validated? Where was God in all of this? How could Jesus's loving Father let him die on a cross? How could the brutal death of Jesus on a cross be an act of atonement, wiping away the sins of humanity? Even reference to the suffering servant passages of Isaiah, while tying the crucifixion back to Hebrew Scripture, seems an unsatisfying and insufficient explanation.

Clearly, resurrection was one solution. Several devoted and some non-devoted followers, e.g., the persecutor Saul, felt the presence of Jesus after his death. In whatever way you wish to understand the resurrection, the essence of Jesus survived his death. Subsequently, Jewish Christian communities grew in congregants under the guidance of the Jerusalem church and Paul's work among the Gentiles. The resurrection was vindication, but the human need for understanding led to all kinds of explanations as to who Jesus was and how he was a savior. All of this analysis occurred within the framework or matrix of the ancient cultic mind of sacrifice. In the process of forming an understanding of Jesus's saving capacity within this framework, the atonement theologies were born and revised over the centuries.

An exhaustive discussion of the development of atonement theologies is beyond the scope of this chapter and many fine resources are available for a more complete overview.[2] Nor will we be able to survey the various contentions of groups attempting to understand Jesus's divinity yet human-ity. However, we shall proceed with a discussion of some biblical references that underlie atonement theology and some of the major subsequent devel-opments that are still with us today.

New Testament Bases for Atonement Doctrines

The earliest New Testament Canonical Scriptures were written by the Apos-tle Paul. He never knew Jesus while Jesus was alive and he spent little time describing Jesus's earthly life or recounting Jesus's teachings. Paul was na-scent Christianity's chief marketer, spreading Christianity throughout the major cities of the Roman Empire. Unlike Jesus whose ministry, until the last few weeks, focused on the rural areas of Galilee, Paul took Christianity to the metropolis, a strategic shift that dominated the Christian movement for millennia and mostly left rural peasants adrift.[3] This strategy was very successful and with only as few a thousand Christians in the empire in the year 40 CE it grew to into the millions by 300 CE. An average annual

2. For example, see Wink, *Human Being*, 104–11.

3. Stark, *Triumph of Christianity*, 262–63.

growth rate of 3 percent and the nurturing Christian lifestyle resulted in Christians becoming an increasingly larger portion of the empire's rather stagnant overall population growth.[4]

Paul was a masterful writer. While he could present his arguments in a straightforward manner, he was also adept at the use of metaphor. One need only read his prose in 1 Cor 13:1, "If I speak in the tongues of mortals and of angels, but do not have love, I am a noisy gong or a clanging cymbal," or his analogy of the body of Christ being as a human body in 1 Cor 12:12–27, to understand this.

Examples pertinent to atonement include 1 Cor 5:7–8, "For our paschal lamb, Christ, has been sacrificed. Therefore, let us celebrate the festival, not with the old yeast, the yeast of malice and evil, but with the unleavened bread of sincerity and truth." Here Paul likens Christ to the paschal lamb that is sacrificed on the eve of Passover. While clearly a cultic reference he moves to speak not of celebrating the festival with traditional cultic ritual, but rather with the unleavened bread of sincerity and truth. Later in Rom 3:23–25 he wrote, "Since all have sinned and fall short of the glory of God; they are now justified by his grace as a gift, through the redemption that is in Christ Jesus, whom God put forward as a sacrifice of atonement by his blood, effective through faith." Paul again draws upon the cultic analogy of blood purification and appeasement in Rom 5:9 when he writes, "Now that we have been justified by his blood, will we be saved through him from the wrath of God." Paul used whatever metaphor to which his audience would relate, not even avoiding mixing metaphors at times. Did Paul mean for any of this to be taken literally? Or was he using these metaphors to express the meaning of Jesus's mission in ways that people of the first century would understand?

Paul was not alone. The Gospels also contributed to this. In Mark 10:45 we have, "For the son of man came not to be served but to serve, and to give his life a ransom for many." Matthew, probably using Mark as a resource, repeated the concept in Matt 20:28. Later the idea of ransom was restated in 1 Tim 2:6. Additionally, Eph 5:2 brings in the metaphor of sacrifice with an aroma pleasing to God and reference to blood redemption. It reads, "Therefore be imitators of God, as beloved children, and live in love, as Christ loved us and gave himself up for us, a fragrant offering and sacrifice to God," and then in Eph 1:7, "In him we have redemption through his blood, the forgiveness of our trespasses, according to the riches of his grace."

---

4. Ibid., 156–65.

Alluding to the Day of Atonement and the cultic atonement sacrifice, Heb 9:24–28 reads as follows, "For Christ did not enter a sanctuary made by human hands, a mere copy of the true one, but he entered into heaven itself, now to appear in the presence of God on our behalf. Nor was it to offer himself again and again, as the high priest enters the Holy Place year after year with blood that is not his own; for then he would have had to suffer again and again since the foundation of the world. But as it is, he has appeared once for all at the end of the age to remove sin by the sacrifice of himself. And just as it is appointed for mortals to die once, and after that the judgment, so Christ, having been offered once to bear the sins of many, will appear a second time, not to deal with sin, but to save those who are eagerly waiting for him."

In these densely packed sentences the author introduces Christ as the counter to the Day of Atonement, sacrificing himself to remove sin once and for all, bearing the sins of many, and in doing so acting as an intermediary on our behalf. Further in Heb 10:10 the author repeats that our sin is removed once and for all by Jesus's death

First John 1:1–2 reiterates these concepts with, "But if anyone does sin, we have an advocate with the Father, Jesus Christ the righteous; and he is the atoning sacrifice for our sins, and not for ours only but also for the sins of the whole world." Then in John 1:7 we have, "But if we walk in the light as he himself is in the light, we have fellowship with one another, and the blood of Jesus, his son, cleanses us from all sin." And later in John 4:10, "In this is love, not that we loved God but that he loved us and sent his son to be the atoning sacrifice for our sins." In 1 Pet 1:18–19 we have, "You know that you were ransomed from the futile ways inherited from your ancestors, not with perishable things like silver or gold, but with the precious blood of Christ, like that of a lamb without defect or blemish."

At this point we have the ancient cultic concepts of ransom, transference of sin, atoning sacrifice, blood purification, and redemption or payment forming a basis, when taken literally, for the doctrine of atonement to flourish. Next we will briefly review some of the main characters in the development of these doctrines.

Much of the Christian leadership left Jerusalem in the late 60s CE to relocate in the Decapolis as it became clear that Jerusalem was about to fall to the Romans, as it ultimately did in 70 CE. The Decapolis was a place of safety as it was Hellenized and aligned with Rome. For example, it is thought that the Johannine Community, that authored the Gospel of John, is believed to have gone into exile there prior to relocating to Ephesus. With Christian leadership in the Decapolis and beyond, conditions were in place for the Christian movement to proceed in Gentile country, where Paul had laid a foundation. But how was atonement to be understood? Would the Greek-influenced society understand the nuances of Paul and others? Perhaps not. As Stephen Finlan has put it, "Paul cannot be blamed for the very literal minded and morbid theologies that lesser minds have developed, but we also cannot deny that these theologies grew out of Pauline tradition."[5] Bishop Spong contends that the metaphoric Jewish prose of the New Testament was incomprehensible to the literally minded Gentile theologians. As a result, "Absent this context, these Gentiles began to literalize the Jesus stories, a practice which the original writers of the Gospels could never have imagined."[6]

Attempts to Unravel the Mystery

So the questions became, "What's this all about?" Did God set Jesus up to be murdered? How does the death of Jesus save us all? Was Jesus sacrificed to atone for our sins? Was Jesus the perfect unblemished substitute sacrificed in place of us? These are some of the lingering questions that the Gentile theologians sought to answer within their literal frame of reference. This is the backdrop for the theories of atonement subsequently developed.

Denny Weaver has classified the explanations for atonement into three categories,[7] which Finlan and Wink have largely adopted. The earliest has been called *Christus Victor*. This view held sway for the first millennium, though there were critiques of it, at least around the edges. Christus Victor had two forms. According to Weaver, in the ransom version Satan was believed to hold the souls of humanity captive. In a contractual agreement God handed over the life of Jesus as a ransom payment for human souls. By raising Jesus from the dead, God tricked Satan and thus triumphed over the devil and the souls of humans were released from his captivity. Thus, the name Christus Victor or Christ the Victor. A second version features a cosmic battle between God and Satan. In this conflict Jesus was killed, but his resurrection proved God's supremacy over the forces of evil.

5. Finlan, *Problems with Atonement*, 62.

6. Spong, *Biblical Literalism*, 41.

7. Weaver, "Violence," 150–76.

In the Christus Victor model there are three actors: God, Satan, and humanity. Like all periods when Scriptures were written or theologians wrote about them, this model was influenced by the overriding themes of the cultural milieu. In this case it was the Latin advances in the legal system. In Christus Victor, "Salvation takes on the pattern of the Roman idea of rewards and punishments, legal process, and the role of intercessors in court."[8]

By the eleventh century dissatisfaction surfaced with the Christus Victor theory. Anselm, a Benedictine monk, philosopher, and theologian devised what has become known as the satisfaction theory of atonement. Anselm lived his adult life in the last half of the eleventh century, born in 1033, died in 1109. In this formulation, Satan is taken out of the equation and what is left is God and humanity. Under this concept of atonement God's honor is offended by human sin which upsets the order of the cosmos. The death of Jesus as the son of God restored God's honor and the order of the cosmos.[9] As with the Latin theologians, his theory was heavily influenced by the social milieu of his day. In the medieval feudal system, if a vassal sinned against the lord of the manor, the lord's honor would take a hit that could only be restored by some sacrifice on the part of the offender.

Protestant reformers built upon this to emphasize the idea of penal substitution. "For them, Jesus's death satisfied the divine law's requirement that sin be punished. Thus with his death, Jesus submitted to and bore the punishment that was really due to us—humankind—as sinners. Jesus was punished in our place. Jesus substituted himself for us, and died a penal, substitutionary death."[10] Could there be any clearer application of the scapegoat practice of the ancient world? Since we are all sinful, only the perfect, unblemished Jesus could make this sacrifice on our behalf. Hence, the ancient concept of sacrifice and Paul's metaphor of Jesus dying for our sins is literally invoked and it remains very much with us today.

Still another theory of atonement with roots in the Epistle to the Hebrews was authored by Abelard. He was a French philosopher and theologian born in 1079 and died in 1142. Abelard was appalled by Anselm's contention that Jesus had to die for God's honor to be restored and instead postulated that God gave his only son as a sacrifice because of his love for humanity. Wink has called this the love theory, while others refer to it as the moral

---

8. Finlan, *Problems with Atonement*, 70.

9. Weaver, "Violence" 152.

10. Ibid.

influence theory of atonement. In this case, "God the Father shows love to us sinners by giving us his most precious possession, his son, to die for us."[11] Here is a reversal of cultic practice in which sinners sacrifice a valued possession to appease God. In this case God sacrifices his most valued possession out of love to be reconciled with humanity. While this may sound more enlightened, it still left us with a God who put his own son on the butcher block.

A century later John Duns Scotus (1266–1308), the Franciscan philosopher and theologian, authored the acceptance theory of atonement. In this theory God arbitrarily chooses through the life of Jesus to more fully reveal the character of divinity. The life and death of Jesus illustrates the enduring love of God even in the face of the inhumanity that led to the cross. Thus Jesus illustrates and teaches us what it means to be fully human and what God's desire is for us human beings to become. Following this path is how one becomes *at-one-ment* with God. Consistent with this approach, Fr. Richard Rohr has written, "Jesus wasn't changing God's mind about us, but, rather, he was changing our mind about God."[12]

Taking Stock

Let's take a deep breath and review where we have been. Earlier we found the following themes in the ancient Old Testament cult of sacrifice: (1) aromatic appeasement; (2) burnt offerings of unblemished livestock bringing forgiveness; (3) blood cleansing and purification; (4) scapegoating; and (5) paying a ransom. In the New Testament we found comparison to the cultic practices such as: (1) Christ as a fragrant sacrifice; (2) Christ as the sacrificial lamb and unblemished sacrifice; (3) Christ's sacrifice bringing redemption, blood cleansing, and atonement; (4) Christ as bearer of the sins of many; and (5) Christ as ransom payment for many. In all of this Christ acts as the intermediary and atoning sacrifice for our sins.

The earliest atonement theory, Christus Victor focused on the ransom, Christ as the ultimate unblemished sacrifice and his role as an intermediary between all reflecting the legal concepts of the Roman Empire. Anselm's later satisfaction theory, influenced by the feudal society of his time, said that human sin dishonored God and that humanity could not right this grievance, only the sacrifice of the perfect unblemished son of God could do so. Protestant reformers ran with this and added that Jesus bore the

11. Ibid., 153.

12. Rohr, *Dancing Standing Still*, Kindle location 1079.

punishment in our place (a reference to the scapegoating) which became known as the penal substitutionary atonement. The moral influence theory of Abelard removed God's honor from atonement and proposed that God so loved humanity that he gave his most precious possession, his son, to die for us. While this made God less wrathful, it also left him as child abuser in chief. These approaches still leave us with concepts of cultic sacrifice and atonement through the death and blood of Jesus. John Duns Scotus's acceptance theory, on the other hand, provides an approach that moves beyond cultic thinking. Unfortunately, this theory has taken a backseat to the more brutal conceptualization and explanations.

Could Jesus Actually Endorse the Sacrificial Cult Explanations for His Death?

As Paul's literalized theology became dominant one must wonder, if he had written more about Jesus's teachings, would all this cultic influenced atonement theology have happened? For Jesus himself, cultic practices were not his primary concern. Drawing on Jer 7:11, did Jesus not insinuate that the Temple priests were making the Temple into a den of robbers as reported in Mark 11:17 and repeated in Matt 21:13 and Luke 19:46? Did Jesus not challenge the sincerity and efficacy of the Pharisees who advocated cultic purity outlined in the tradition of the elders as their path to salvation?

An often over-sentimentalized passage recounted in Luke 21:1–4 reads, "He looked up and saw rich people putting their gifts into the treasury; he also saw a poor widow put in two small copper coins. He said, 'Truly I tell you, this poor widow has put in more than all of them; for all of them have contributed out of their abundance, but she out of her poverty has put in all she had to live on.'" But the Torah was quite clear that the obligation was for rich and poor alike to contribute a half shekel to the Sanctuary annually, as we have indicated earlier. This passage not only praises the poor widow for giving all she had, but also flies in the face of the Temple cult's half shekel annual atonement ransom payment.

Jesus is clearly in conflict with the two bastions of cultism: the Sadducees who ran the Temple cult and the Pharisees who promoted the purity rituals. In several cases he told people that their sins were forgiven. Only once did he suggest that someone present themselves to the Temple priests and that was to show them that Jesus had healed the victim's leprosy. Further, as the theologian Elisabeth Schüssler Fiorenza has pointed out, "The central symbolic actualization of the *basileia* vision of Jesus is not the cultic meal but the festive table of a royal banquet or wedding feast."[13] Why then would credence be given to sacrificial cultic interpretation of Jesus's death when he himself downplayed such ritual and those who perpetuated it?

The only answers is that, as with Paul, using the familiar cultic practices as reference points made sense to the ancient mind. Once they were instituted they became literalized and cast in concrete. Out of that literalization emanated the blood atonement theories that are still very much alive with us today. One need only consider blood themed Christian hymns to see this. Some are still present in mainline Christian churches, such as "Nothing but the Blood" by Robert Lowry (1826–1899) and "There Is a Fountain Filled with Blood" by William Cowper (1731–1800).[14] Hardly a Sunday passes that reference is not made to Jesus dying for our sins. In some churches you will hear that his blood washed us clean as snow. But did he die for our sins? Did his blood have cleansing power? Is there an alternative to understanding atonement, i.e., drawing closer to God, apart from a cultic framework?

A Twenty-First Century Atonement

Moving away from the ancient cultic notion of atonement rests on how we conceptualize Scripture, God, and humanity. First, is Scripture the literal word of God or is it the narrative of humanity seeking to describe their understanding of the divine? Second, is God a wrathful deity of conditional compassion requiring sacrifice and payback, or a loving and unconditionally compassionate deity? Third is humanity deprived and hopelessly sinful, a perversion of God's original perfect creation, or is humanity a work in process, with the potential to evolve into a Jesus-like full humanity?

If Scripture is the literal infallible word of God, we have a very difficult path to follow. As we look at Scripture, we can find depictions of God as wrathful and genocidal, ordering the annihilation of entire communities and wreaking retribution on those breaking the covenant. And this is not just an Old Testament phenomenon. The New Testament contains similar confusing characterizations. Scripture viewed as humanity's best attempts to describe their experience and understanding of God opens the opportunity to choose which depiction best fits one's own experience. If that is a God of wrath and jealousy, then the blood sacrifice theories of atonement,

13. Schüssler Fiorenza, *In Memory of Her*, 119.

14. United Methodist Church, *United Methodist Hymnal*, 362, 622.

based on the ancient cultic practices, are likely appropriate. However, if God is viewed as Jesus depicted the deity, then the whole blood atonement theories just create an enigma. Isn't it time, in this twenty-first century to move beyond the ancient cultic mind-set?

What one believes about Scripture and the nature of God also influences how one thinks about humanity. It is clear that evil exists in the world. It is also clear that human beings are preoccupied with their own welfare and that oftentimes this leads to hurt and broken relationships, individually and collectively. But there is evidence all around us that things evolve from the fundamental to the sophisticated. Is humankind hopelessly sinful, born in sin? Perhaps, but it seems that an uplifting understanding of humanity as just not yet being fully human, but with the potential of becoming so, leads to a more helpful and uplifting theology.

Conclusion

I believe Jesus was an atoning presence—not in the cultic sense it has been portrayed, but rather in the sense of John Duns Scotus's acceptance theory. It was God's intent to more fully reveal divine nature through the incarnate life of Jesus, not to get payment, restore honor, or to be appeased through a cultic blood sacrifice. As Schüssler Fiorenza has put it, "The suffering and death of Jesus, like that of John and all the other prophets sent to Israel before him, are not required in order to atone for the sins of the people in the face of an absolute God, but are the result of violence against the envoys of Sophia, i.e., wisdom, who proclaim God's unlimited goodness and the equality and election of all her children."[15] Jesus's death was brutal and we still play a role in it to the extent we focus inward on our own self-absorbed concerns and ignore his call to live in love for one another and the common good. If we pursue a self-focused lifestyle that clings to outdated thought processes, submits to bullying, knuckles under to injustice, and seeks to gain or retain power and advancement at the expense of others, we are guilty of his death surely as much as those who brutalized and crucified him two thousand years ago. It is in Jesus's understanding of the God he called Abba that we get a true insight into a deity of unconditional love that wills for us to become fully human as Jesus was fully human. When we accept this understanding and pursue a compatible lifestyle we can be in tune with God and at-one-ment with the divine.

15. Schüssler Fiorenza, *In Memory of Her*, 135.

6

Is Jesus the Only Way?

Jesus answered, "I am the way and the truth and the life.
No one comes to the Father except through me."

JOHN 14:6

JOHN 14:6 HAS PERHAPS caused more heartburn and interreligious quarrels
than any other verse in the New Testament Scriptures. "No one comes to
the Father except through me." Does this mean as so many people interpret
it, that no other religion is valid and that Christianity has a corner on the
God market? Does it mean, as many fundamentalist and biblical literalists
believe, that only those who accept Jesus as their lord and savior will spend
eternity with God while those who don't will be condemned to hell? Is Jesus
the only way, the only path to God?

Scholars believe that John is the last of the Gospels to be written. Not
only is John the latest Gospel, but it also has significant difference with the
Gospels of Mark, Matthew, and Luke. These latter three Gospels are called
the Synoptic Gospels because of their similarities in the biographical depiction of Jesus's life. Some have referred to John as the spiritual Gospel, more
mystical and theological than the Synoptics. It contains many Christians' fa-
vorite Scriptures and its passages are often read at funeral services. We do not
know who wrote the Gospel of John. It had been thought over the centuries
that John, the beloved disciple, was the author as attested to in John 21:20.
Contemporary scholarship shows that the Gospel was written and redacted
over a period of time, perhaps as many as three times. The earliest drafts

could have originated either in oral or written forms by a beloved disciple if that person actually existed. There has been considerable controversy regarding the identity of the beloved disciple, including the possibility that this disciple was a literary construction on behalf of all those who followed the selfless path of Jesus.[1] However, in spite of controversy and disagreements, there are some areas of consensus. Scholars for the most part believe that (1) even the earliest parts of John were written after the fall of Jerusalem; (2) the finished version appeared around the end of the first century, 90–100 CE; (3) the author(s) were Jews; and (4) the final version was written in the Diaspora, possibly in Ephesus. Regarding the last part, while perhaps written in Ephesus, the author(s) have a detailed knowledge of Jerusalem and the earliest author was likely part of the Jesus movement in Jerusalem prior to its destruction in 70 CE. But we will say more about this later.

To interpret "no one comes to the Father except through me," we need to consider several issues. First, who wrote the Gospel and why did they write it? Second, how did the Jesus story mesh with traditional Judaism? Third, how did the Gospel differ from the Synoptic Gospels, Mark, Matthew, and Luke? Fourth, what were the major religious groups of the time and what was their relationship to the Gospel writers. These are the matters we turn to next.

Who Wrote It and Why Did They Write It?

The Gospel of John was written by the leadership of a community of Jewish Christians that became known as the Johannine community. It probably began as an oral tradition; perhaps as early as the 30s CE. Scholars for the most part agree that the Gospel of John developed over a long period of time. Evidence is that it was redacted or revised on at least three occasions and was completed late in the first century, probably in the mid-nineties. Its early layers were probably written in Palestine by the leadership of the Johannine community. As indicated, it was completed in the Diaspora. It was written to express the Johannine understanding of Jesus, which, as we will see shortly, differed from the Christian literature that was already in existence.

Raymond Brown, who has written extensively on the Johannine community following the lead of Bultmann and Wellhausen, contends that the Gospel contains not only the community's theological positions, but also insights into the community's history and struggles.[2] It is widely understood

1. Spong, *Fourth Gospel*, 250–53.
2. Brown, *Community of the Beloved Disciple*, 17.

that the Johannine community began as a community of Jews, including many followers of John the Baptist, who came to believe that Jesus was the Messiah, the one that Moses promised would come to the Israelites.[3] Sometime prior to the fall of Jerusalem and Rome's destruction of the Temple, it is believed that for safety reasons the community relocated to a city in the Decapolis, a Greco-Roman collection of ten cities east of the Jordan River. Many believe they settled with other fleeing Christians in the city of Pella and the exodus from Jerusalem occurred in the time frame of 66–67 CE. During this period the Romans were least active in the region and the rebel Jews had some military successes.[4] Brown and others believe the story of Jesus converting the Samaritan woman at the well in John 4 is an indication that the Johannine community had begun converting and accepting non-Jews into their community, of which there would be plenty in the region. Later references to Greeks wishing to see Jesus in John 12:20–21 has also been interpreted as evidence of the acceptance and conversion of Gentiles into the Johannine community. By this time the community had taken on the view that it is not birthright that determines who the real Christians are, but rather their belief about who Jesus was, thus accommodating their non-Jewish converts. After the fall of Jerusalem some of the Christian groups who had left Jerusalem for the safety of the Decapolis returned. However, the evidence seems to point in the direction that the Johannine community departed for the Diaspora and therefore the final version of John is likely to have been written in Ephesus. Perhaps the diversity in the group would have made them less welcome in Jerusalem.

As the community matured it became bolder in its claims about Jesus. That, along with its acceptance and inclusion of non-Jews, brings it into substantial conflict with the less pluralistic Pharisaic Judaism emerging after the destruction of the Temple. This may well have led them to become *personae-non-gratae* in the synagogues while many other Christian groups continued worshipping in the synagogues for centuries.[5] In many ways the community began to see itself as practicing the only true religion among the many forms available in the Greco-Roman culture and certainly among the varieties of Christianity. Thus, the Gospel was written by members of this community to express their understanding of Jesus, reinforce this belief within the community, and promulgate it to likely converts.

3. Deut 18:18.

4. van Houwelingen, "Fleeing Forward," 181–200.

5. Fredriksen, "Christians in the Roman Empire," 597.

The Jesus Story and Jewish Tradition

Is the Jesus story so far afield of Jewish understanding of their faith tradition in the first century to be a scandal unto the Jews? As the Gospels were written, it seems clear that tensions existed from the beginning of Jesus's ministry between him and certain Jewish groups. Yet he also had his followers among the Jews. Rabbi Daniel Boyarin contends that "the theology of the Gospels, far from being a radical innovation within Israelite religious tradition, is a highly conservative return to the very most ancient moments within that tradition, moments that had been largely suppressed in the meantime—but not entirely." He goes on to say, "According to Mark (and Matthew even more so), far from abandoning the laws and practices of the Torah, Jesus was a staunch defender of the Torah against what he perceived to be threats to it from the Pharisees."[6] Reed points out that even Jesus's critique of purity practices was not aimed at the practice itself, but at the lack of the Pharisees' integrity in practicing the purity laws they were promulgating.[7] Others also argue for the devout Jewishness of Jesus.[8]

The Pharisees were promulgating a reform of Judaism possibly developed during the Exile in Babylon, which was a verbal teaching they called the tradition of the elders. We first encountered this in chapter 3. According to Boyarin, "Jesus's Judaism was a conservative reaction against some radical innovations in the Law and social developments stemming from Pharisees and Scribes of Jerusalem. . . . Jesus was not fighting against Judaism, but rather within it. . . . The only controversy surrounding Jesus was whether . . . [he] truly was the one for whom the Jews were waiting."[9] Obviously a small group believed so, and the larger group did not. This may explain Jesus's popularity in the outer regions of Galilee where he criticized Antipas's urbanization, monetization, and Hellenization of Galilee with teachings favoring the return of self-sufficiency, sabbatical restoration, and economic justice for all, as well as his opposition from the Jerusalem crowd's new teachings and snobbish holding of Galileans in a state of disdain. Regarding the scandal of crucifixion Boyarin concludes that "although there is precious little pre-Christian evidence among Jews for the suffering of the

---

6. Boyarin, *Jewish Gospels*, Kindle location 125.

7. Reed, *Archaeology and the Galilean Jesus*, 57.

8. Charlesworth and Aviam, "Reconstructing First-Century Galilee," 130–31.

9. Boyarin, *Jewish Gospels*, Kindle location 1551.

Messiah, there are good reasons to consider this too no stumbling block for the Jewishness of the ideas about the Jesus Messiah as well."[10]

Boyarin goes on to argue that traditional scholarship had concluded that the suffering servant passages in Isa 53 did not pertain to a messiah, but rather to the nation of Israel as a whole. But current scholarship has discovered that until the modern times many Jewish authorities read Isa 53 as being about the Messiah and it was just in the last few centuries that it was read allegorically. If Boyarin is correct and increasingly his views are taking hold, then the argument and place of Jesus was not so much a revolutionary attack on Judaism as it was a call to return to the true nature of Judaism and their God. Rather than a break with Judaism, Christianity, for those who believed Jesus was the Messiah, was a continuous unfolding story of divine revelation and reform resulting in a return to the earlier essence of Judaism and eschewing the legalisms of Pharisaic teachings.

How is the Gospel of John Different?

If the Jesus story is not so foreign to Jewish tradition, then why did the Gospel of John create such a stir among certain Jewish groups and how does it differ from the Synoptic Gospels? In this section we will focus on three key departures from the Synoptic Gospels. The first is John's formulation of Christology. The second is the polemics against the Jews. The third is the widespread use of metaphor.

Christology

There is consensus among scholars that Mark was the first Gospel written followed by Matthew, Luke, and then finally by John. As successive Gospels were written there was a move toward embellishment. John is at the apex of this embellishment. As the Gospel takes shape, it takes on a higher Christology than the previously written Scriptures. In John's prologue we encounter Jesus not being divine at the resurrection as Paul believed, nor adopted by God at his baptism as Mark believed, nor at his unique birth as Matthew and Luke wrote, but he was always divine, being the logos or "word of God" that existed since the beginning of time. He was the light of the world and the darkness could not snuff out the light. In John, Jesus

10. Ibid., Kindle location 1876.

becomes not only the son of God, but God. Consider just two examples where the Gospel put these words in Jesus's mouth. In John 14:19 it says, "Whoever has seen me has seen the Father," and in John 8:58 Jesus said, "Very truly, I tell you, before Abraham was, I am." The words "I am" are drawn from Exod 3:14 where God speaks to Moses at the burning bush and self-identifies as "I am." Clearly the Gospel of John held Jesus to a higher level of Christology than did the Synoptic Gospels.

Polemics Against the Jews

Equating Jesus with God is what gave the Jews such heartburn. It had been believed by many that this began the period of hostilities between Christians and Jews in general that lasted for centuries. This seemed a reasonable conclusion to draw, for example, from Paul's account in 2 Cor 11:24 of "five times I have received from the Jews the forty lashes minus one" and by projecting chronologically backwards from the hostilities that began after the Council at Nicaea in 325 CE. However, recent scholarship has begun to reconsider the relationship that existed between Jews and Christians at this time. Toward the end of the first century, the Temple in Jerusalem, which was central to the Jews' religious identity, had been destroyed but the rabbinic replacement had not yet been firmly established. Further, about 85 CE the Sanhedrin had been reestablished and the Jewish teaching center at Jamnia issued an edict that Christians be expelled from the synagogues. Martyn's exegesis of John 9:22, in which fear of the Jewish leaders by parents of the healed blind man was interpreted as a subtext for animosity between Jews and Christians late in the first century, further advanced this view of hostile relations between Jews and Christians.[11]

Yet contemporary scholarship is painting a different picture. This picture reveals that the early tensions were not Jew against Christian, but rather tensions within the Jewish family regarding threads of thought that long preceded the life of Jesus.[12] I once heard a rabbi say that "whenever two Jews gather there are three opinions." Apparently this is not a twenty-first-century phenomena, but rather a time honored practice of questioning and debate that has been characteristic of Jewry since antiquity. Indeed, it seems more the case now that Christians and synagogue followers had a simpatico relationship well beyond the first few centuries of the Common

11. Klink, "Expulsion from the Synagogue?," 99–118.

12. Boyarin, *Jewish Gospels*, Kindle location 1532.

Era and differences with Christians and Jews were differences of opinion within the Jewish tradition. For example, Daniel Boyarin has written, "Judaism and Christianity in this period shared crisscrossing lines of history and religious development. . . . One could travel, metaphorically, from Rabbinic Jew to Christian along a continuum where one would hardly know where one stopped and the other began."[13] He believes that the banishment of Christians from the synagogue is much overblown and was never successfully carried out. During this period Judaism was in disarray and it would be centuries before either Christianity or Judaism took a form that clearly distinguished them from one another.

But was this necessarily the case for the Johannine community? John 5–12 is replete with conflict between Jesus and the "Jews." Read as a subtext for the experience of the Johannine community it does reflect hostile relations between the Jewish authorities and the Johannine community. Could it have been that the Johannine community pushed their Christology to a level unacceptable to the synagogue leaders that led to expulsion for this Christian community, but was never enforced for other Jewish Christian groups? Such a scenario would reconcile Martyn's exegesis of John 9:22 with the later scholarship.

As the Johannine community became estranged from their Jewish roots they took in more non-Jewish converts and developed an attitude of what Brown describes as a universal dualism. The idea was advanced that the true children of God were those who believed that Jesus was divine and even equal to God. The community became open to all who "believed in his name." But there was still the dualism of light and darkness, and of those who believed and those who did not believe, the insiders and the outsiders. Those who believed they were the children of God regardless of whether or not they were of Abraham's blood line. But those on the outside were the children of darkness. This is exactly the tack one would expect as the community and Jewish authorities distance themselves from one another. Tension between the community and the Jews is further evidenced by the sixty-one references to Jews in John's Gospel. While not all are negative, a great many are and are in a very damning sense. By comparison, the word "Jews" only appears fourteen times in all three of the Synoptic Gospels combined.

13. Eliav, "Jews and Judaism," 569–70.

Metaphor

The authors of the Gospel of John make extensive use of allegory and metaphor. Examples include John 1:4–5, where Jesus is depicted as the light that shines in the darkness. In John 4:10–11 and John 7:38 Jesus depicts the Spirit of God as living water. In John 6:35 Jesus declares that he is the bread of life. Clearly, Jesus is neither light nor water nor bread. These are literary constructions to express deeper meanings.

Bishop Spong notes that the authors of John illustrate the folly of taking this Gospel literally rather than metaphorically.[14] The Gospel is as Michael Brown says like a Sherlock Holmes story. In these stories Watson is set up as the one who is dense, the reader has some greater insight, but Holmes is clearly the one who resolves the bewilderment.[15] The author of John sets up a literary character who acts as Watson, you and I as the reader see through the character's foolishness, and Jesus is the Holmes who knows all. Consider Jesus's encounter with Nicodemus in John 3:3–5. Jesus says that "to enter the kingdom of God one must be born from above." The author has Nicodemus confused, missing the point, and mulling over how he can go back into his mother's womb to be born again. In John 4:7–15 Jesus meets a Samaritan woman at the well. He says to her, "Everyone who drinks of this water will be thirsty again, but those who drink of the water that I will give them will never be thirsty." She replies, "how can you give me living water, you don't even have a bucket." Clearly, Nicodemus did not have to go back to his mother's womb nor did Jesus need a bucket at the well to provide the living water. These are all literary constructions to express Johannine theology. The Gospel of John's extensive use of metaphor makes a literal reading of John a fool's errand.

The Major Players and Their Relationship to the Johannine Community

Modern Christians often do not appreciate or understand the complexity of society at the end of the first century and view Christianity as though it always existed as the orthodox Christianity that developed after 325 CE. But in the final years of the first century there were many religious groups with differing allegiances and understandings of the divine. While complete

14. Spong, *Fourth Gospel*, 63.

15. Brown, *Community of the Beloved Disciple*, 89.

coverage of the diversity of religious belief at this time is far beyond the scope of this chapter, several religious viewpoints are important for understanding the Gospel of John. We will address three groups, the pagan culture, the Jews, and the Christians along with some important subgroups.

The Pagans

While approximations and projections are difficult to nail down, it has been estimated that the population of the Roman Empire numbered 50 to 60 million at the end of the first century. About 90 percent were pagans.[16] Additionally the populations were fluid and migration frequent. As a result, the empire was ripe with gods. Temples representing a selection of diverse gods were present in all the major cities. The general population wished to keep on the "good side" of these personal gods by making various animal and grain sacrifices. Consequently, worship was public and took on a defensive posture of appeasement. Keep the gods happy and all will go well, or conversely when problems arise, the gods must be offended and need conciliation.

In the ancient world gods were both regional and ethnic. The expectation was that the populace would worship and pay deference to the gods of the region and to the gods of their particular ethnic heritage. Additionally, all were expected to worship the imperial cult of the reigning Caesar. The exception was for the Jews. First through custom and later written into Roman law, out of respect for the ancient Jewish religion and its widely admired lifestyle, the Jews were exempt from these expectations. They were permitted to worship only their ethnic God, the God of Israel. This was an important distinction with interesting consequences that we will see shortly.

There was a subset of the pagan culture of special interest. They were the God Fearers, a group of pagan Gentiles that was attracted to the synagogue, fascinated with monotheism, and admired the Jews' moralistic lifestyle. We first encountered them in chapter 2. While they did not convert to Judaism, they often attended and supported the local synagogues. These God Fearers are likely to have been a source of recruitment for the Johannine community and one group for whom the final version of the Gospel of John was intended to attract. The other pagan groups would likely have been rejected by the community as nonbelievers who preferred "living in darkness." Thus, the Gospel's claim of exclusivity in John 14:6 would provide the hard sell to attract these God Fearers and like sympathizers.

16. Eliav, "Jews and Judaism," 565.

The Jews

Of the approximately 5 million Jews in the empire at this time between 10 and 20 percent lived in Palestine while the remainder lived in Roman cities throughout the Mediterranean region, i.e., the Diaspora. At the end of the first century, the Temple in Jerusalem, which had been central to the Jews' religious identity had been destroyed and the rabbinic replacement had not yet been firmly established. Many Jews attempted to live according to the Jewish tradition as best they understood it. Others became followers of John the Baptist and believed him to be the Messiah. Still others believed that Jesus was the Messiah, but kept quiet about it so as not to cause trouble that might get them expelled from the synagogue. Michael Brown called this latter group Crypto-Christians. There were also those who previously believed Jesus was the Messiah, but then reverted back to traditional Judaism and worshipped in the synagogues.

One could also draw a distinction between the Jews of Palestine and the Jews of the Diaspora. The Christian historian, Paul Johnson, described the differences this way. Jews of Judea and Galilee "tended to be poor, backward, obscurantist, narrow minded, fundamentalist, and xenophobic; the Diaspora Jews were expansive, rich, cosmopolitan, well-adjusted to Roman norms and to Hellenistic culture, Greek speaking, literate, and open to ideas."[17] The latter acculturated into the Greco-Roman society, serving in local governments, frequenting bath houses, and participating in athletic events. "Diaspora Jews also, to the degree that they engaged in athletics, higher education, the military, civic politics, drama, or music, were involved in activities entwined with the gods of majority culture."[18] The Palestinian Jews, after the fall of Jerusalem and destruction of the Temple, continued to create tensions with the Roman hegemony leading up to the Bar Kokhba Revolt of 132–136 CE. This was the final Jewish revolt. The Romans' response in all practicality was a genocide that decimated the Jewish presence in Palestine. While the Jews of the Diaspora could be a nuisance to the Romans, rebellious Jews in Palestine mounted skirmishes leading up to that final confrontation in 132 CE.

The polemics against the Jews in John were directed at the Palestinian Jews, primarily for their aversion to John's high Christology and expulsion from the synagogues. But far down the list as well they had reason to

17. Johnson, *History of Christianity*, 11.

18. Fredriksen, "Christians in the Roman Empire," 592.

distance themselves because of the Palestinians' rebellious nature. Regarding the Diaspora Jews, tensions with the Johannine community would be centered on how strongly the local synagogues followed directives coming out of Palestine, which undoubtedly varied from location to location.

The Johannine community took a cautious approach to the followers of John the Baptist. They were careful to honor him and recognize his importance, but also to clarify that he was subordinate to Jesus. In John 1:20, John the Baptist has these words attributed to him, "I am not the Messiah," and further in John 1:26–27, "I baptize with water. Among you stands one whom you do not know, the one who is coming after me; I am not worthy to untie the thong of his sandal." The exclusive path to the Father being addressed in John 14:6 was at least partially written to convince this group that Jesus, not John, was the Messiah and the only path to the Father.

Christians

Among the Christian groups we make distinctions between Jewish Christians, non-Jewish Converts, and Crypto-Christians. As we have seen, the Johannine community was initially a community of Jewish Christians. But by the time the Gospel was completed it also contained non-Jewish converts. These later groups resulted in further distance being created between the Jewish authorities and the Johannine community. Brown notes that John 5–12 contains polemics against the Jews, but that there is a shift in John 14–17 to condemnation of the nonbelieving world in general. Earlier we noted that Greco-Roman custom and religious expectation was that citizens would publicly worship regional gods, their own ethnic gods, and the imperial cult. Jews were exempt from this requirement. That meant that Christian Jews were exempt. But non-Jewish Christians were not exempt. They were caught up in a difficult situation, worshipping only the one true God and not worshipping the other gods in the culture. They became the ones subjected to sporadic persecution and martyrdom. Whenever there were bad crop yields, floods, earthquakes, etc., it was assumed the local and ethnic gods were angry. The god's anger was blamed on the Gentile Christian's refusal to worship these local, ethnic, and imperial gods. Paula Fredriksen put it this way:

> The problem, then, in the view of majority culture, was not that gentile Christians were Christians. The problem was that, whatever religious practices these people chose to assume, they were

still, nonetheless, "gentiles." . . . From roughly the end of the first century until 250 CE, these Christians could be the object of local resentments and anxieties precisely because they were not honoring the gods upon whom their city's prosperity depended. . . . Jewish Christians were not so persecuted, because as Jews their exemption from public cult was ancient, traditional, and protected by long legal precedent.[19]

It would appear that with the presence of non-Jewish Christians in the Johannine community being subject to periodic persecution, the shift in polemic focus toward the Jews to the more global polemic toward the broader culture was natural and inevitable.

Brown contends that relations with the Jewish Christians whom he called the apostolic church and Crypto-Christians were more measured. The apostolic church was the church following the teachings found in the earlier gospels and the epistles. Brown distinguishes between them and the Johannine community in terms of those following the teachings of the Apostles versus those following the revelation received from the spirit. The Johannine community honored the apostolic church while at the same time taking a position of superior insight into the nature of Jesus. Eventually, centuries later they seem to rule the day as many parts of the Gospel, unfortunately taken literally, were incorporated into the creeds of orthodoxy.

Crypto-Christians were those who believed Jesus was the Messiah, but chose to do so quietly and remain worshipping in the synagogues. The Johannine community's desire was through the Gospel to embolden the Crypto-Christians to take a stand and to win over those in the apostolic church to their higher christological views. Hence the exclusivity claims of John 14:6 were written to encourage this.

Clearly the late first century was a complex time with many religious groups vying for dominance. The Gospel of John then grew out of these tensions and sought to develop a mystical theology that would sustain this community in its search for grounding in its Jesus movement.

Conclusion

John 14:6 appears toward the end of Jesus's earthly ministry. The disciples had been gathered for a meal, Jesus washes their feet and predicts his betrayal and Peter's denials. He tells his disciples that he is going to prepare

19. Ibid., 602–5.

the way for them. It is now that Jesus is made to declare that he and God are of the same nature. In John 14:6–7 Jesus says, "I am the way and the truth and the life. No one comes to the Father except through me. If you really know me, you will know my Father as well. From now on, you do know him and have seen him." It is shortly thereafter that Jesus is arrested, goes before Pontius Pilot and is crucified.

Scholars have debated whether many of the sayings in John were actually said by Jesus or whether they were put into Jesus's mouth by the post-Easter Johannine authors. We have seen that statements attributed to Jesus not only expressed the community's understanding of who Jesus was to them, but also provides us with a subtext to understanding the experiences of the community itself. The Jesus Seminar, a group of scholars who have extensively studied the Gospels, have developed a methodology to determine which biblical passages the Jesus of history may actually have said versus those that the later Christian community put into his mouth. They concluded over two decades ago that John 14:6 was not something Jesus would have said.[20]

John 14, in which the exclusivity claim appears, is rich in metaphor. An example includes, "In my Father's house there are many dwelling places." Jesus is going to prepare a way for the disciples. His words indicate that he is taking them on a metaphorical journey. But the disciples say they don't know the way. Jesus says he is "the way." John's thesis is that only Jesus's example for living and dying, and not the ubiquitous pagan worship, nor belief in John the Baptist as the Messiah, nor the Judaism that rejected belief in Jesus, nor any of the other religious options available to them at the end of the first century in the Greco-Roman society will bring them to the kingdom. Only the way expressed in the life of Jesus will.

This analysis is not suggesting that the author(s) of John were trying to deceive or manipulate the truth. I have no doubt that given the situation and genre in which the Gospel was written the authors undoubtedly thought they were accurately presenting the case for Jesus. Given the circumstances and context of the people at whom the Gospel was directed, it was undoubtedly a valid statement. As Paul Knitter, has put it,

> Such language, as scholars of the New Testament point out, is "confessional" language—the way of speaking the early communities of Jesus followers used in order to put into words what they felt about this man who had so affected their lives. . . . It is "love

20. Funk et al., *Five Gospels*, 450.

language." And like all love language, it made spontaneous and abundant use of superlatives and exclusives.[21]

Further, it was directed to the needs of a particular community at a particular time, not for all people of all time or intended to address other religions far beyond or outside the Greco-Roman culture. It seems rather arrogant and inconceivable that we should use John 14:6 to restrict God's love to only those who subscribe to the Jesus story. "In fact, given the diversity of human cultures and the movement of history, it will be probable, maybe even necessary, that there be many teachers, revealers, saviors, each speaking to different cultural or historical contexts, each making known at different and deeper depths of what Christians call the Divine."[22] It has been said that "God created humankind in his image and humankind returned the favor." Precluding God from sending other messengers appropriate to other cultures and other times seems an example of making God in our image. Thus, rather than make exclusivity claims for Christianity based upon John 14:6, let us put it into its context and embrace all people of all world religions who seek nonviolence, peace, justice, and love as the foundations of their lives. Let us open dialogue with them and seek to understand those aspects of God that can further illuminate us as to God's essence and presence among us. It is the way of Jesus.

21. Knitter, *Without Buddha*, 124.
22. Ibid., 122.

7

Scripture: Word of God or Word of Man?

Jesus answered them, "You are wrong,
because you know neither the Scriptures nor the power of God."

MATT 22:29

SCRIPTURE, THE QUESTION IS what to make of it? Matthew 22:23–32, places Jesus in a discussion with a small group of Sadducees. Sadducees were the aristocracy of the day, filling many important positions in the Temple, e.g., serving as high priests and filling essential government assignments. The Sadducees posed a question to Jesus about seven brothers, all of whom died childless one after another. It was a brother's duty to marry his deceased brother's widow and have children for his brother. But since none of the brothers had a child with the woman, they asked Jesus, "In the resurrection, then, whose wife of the seven will she be?" The Sadducees did not believe in resurrection or life after death, so the dilemma posed was an attempt to publicly ridicule Jesus. He answered them and in his reply told them they knew "neither Scripture nor the power of God." But that begs the question for us today: What do we know of Scripture? Are we as ignorant as Jesus accuses the Sadducees of being? How should we read the Bible? Does it contain truth or is it merely a volume of fanciful stories made up centuries ago and maintained by ecclesiastical authority? Is it the word of God or the word of man?

Word of God?

Each Sunday after the offering is taken in our worship service and before the sermon, our liturgist reads the day's Scripture lesson. At the end of the reading the liturgist says, "The word of God for the people of God," and the congregation in unison says, "Thanks be to God." Your church may have the same tradition, if not you are likely to have heard this response while visiting another congregation. But I must ask, is Scripture the word of God? Or is it the word of men and perhaps women thinking they are speaking for or about God? If it is the word of God, then must it also be without error?

Much of our educational system emphasizes memorization of facts such as important historical dates, ideas, and concepts that others preceding us have written into our textbooks. We then repeat what we have memorized on a test that we take over the material. This reassures our teachers that we have read and internalized the information presented to us. It also sticks in our brains that way, at least for some period of time. This is necessary to give us a start at an informed and educated life. We learn by taking in what we read and hear literally. We have been doing this since childhood. Our educational system is quite competent at this task. What our educational system is not as good at is instilling critical thinking in us. That is, when engaging us in critiquing the material, we are questioning it and forming our own understanding. Critical thinking isn't absent from our system and certainly our better teachers and professors encourage and require it. But it is underrepresented in our educational process. Is it then no wonder that when we turn to Scripture we invoke our primary mode of learning and take the Scripture literally? Let's pursue this a bit further.

Christians like to think that God's essence is kindness, compassion, and unchangeable. This man Jesus, who Christians believe is the window through which we get a glimpse of the nature of God tells us to love our neighbor as ourselves. In Matt 5:9 Jesus says, "Blessed are the peacemakers, for they will be called children of God," and in Matt 5:44, "Love your enemies and pray for those who persecute you." First Peter 3:9 tells us, "Do not repay evil for evil or abuse for abuse, but, on the contrary, repay with a blessing." And Jas 3:18 reads, "And a harvest of righteousness is sown in peace for those who make peace." All is fine and good up to this point. But how do we reconcile these thoughts with Josh 10:40, which reads, "So Joshua defeated the whole land, the hill country and the Negeb and the lowland and the slopes, and all their kings; he left no one remaining, but utterly destroyed all that breathed, as the LORD God of Israel commanded."

And this is just one example. The books of Numbers, Deuteronomy, and Joshua are replete with these genocidal forays commanded by God.

Many Christians reconcile this by saying the Old Testament God of the Jews was a vengeful and harsh God. The God of the New Testament is the God of love and compassion. Really? Then how does one reconcile that belief with an unforgiving New Testament God that after separating people, as separating sheep and goats, sends the goats to eternal punishment as in Matt 25:46. Aren't we all goats from time to time? Or consider the wrath of God expressed in Rev 16. Neither of these accounts are hardly a description of a loving, unconditionally compassionate God. Further, how can one reconcile the genocidal episodes with the compassionate command to feed the poor, protect the widow and orphan, and look after the alien found throughout the Old Testament books of Exodus and Deuteronomy, and proclaimed by the prophets Jeremiah, Ezekiel, Zechariah, and Malachi? Either God has one schizophrenic personality or our Scriptures are not the word of God, but rather the attempts of ancient people expressing their vision and understanding of the divine in and for their time and place.

The only reasonable way to understand these contradictory messages, as Marcus Borg has argued, is to read the Bible not as how God saw things, but as how people in their ancient communities over hundreds of years, in different settings, with different worldviews, and in different cultures, understood God. The ancient authors of the Scriptures may have been divinely inspired but they wrote within a particular time and place. They also faced certain problems. One was that God is and always has been beyond description. There is no language that can capture the essence of God. All we have are snippets or glimpses of divinity. Further, these glimpses and snippets of the Holy expressed in Scripture are encased in an understanding laced with ancient worldviews, cultural biases, and primitive knowledge. Such being the case, Scripture is influenced by the era in which it was written, the breadth of knowledge available in that era, and the cultural norms of that period. In short, Scripture is going to contain eternal truth alongside of accounts heavily distorted by personal biases, private agendas, cultural editing, and literary methods that are quite foreign to twenty-first-century readers. For these readers, and those who preceded them, sorting out the truths in Scripture is not a trivial matter.

Now, let's reconsider the genocides of Joshua. Did they really happen? There is practically conclusive archaeological evidence that the genocides of Joshua were mythical episodes of heroic conquest and are not historical fact. The archaeologist, William Dever, after decades of directing field studies and with a comprehensive grasp of archaeological literature concludes,

> The Iron I period, as we would call it, was not characterized by decisive military battles, the wholesale destruction of Canaanite urban centers and the annihilation of the populace, and the triumph by brute force of a group of outsiders. It was characterized, rather, as we now know from intense archaeological investigation, by large-scale socio-economic disruption, major demographic shifts to the hill country frontiers, and by life-and-death struggles between competing ethnic and cultural groups that lasted anywhere from one to two centuries.[1]

Dever believes that the accounts in Judges, which in some cases contradict accounts in Joshua and present a slower and less brutal settling of premonarchical Israel, is closer to the reality of the time.

We must not be confused by Scripture depicting two very different and incompatible pictures of God. Dever points out that some Scripture of this time may be nothing more than an early attempt to provide a nationalistic mythology to build the Israelites' confidence in Yahweh's power and provide legitimacy for rightful ownership of the land of Judea. The genocidal episodes are not an accurate characterization of God. In short, understanding Scripture requires us to at least comprehend the context of the time and purpose for which it was written. Reading Scripture as the absolute word of God rather than the words of humans trying to understand the divine is misleading and perhaps even dangerous.

Holy Metaphor

One Sunday not long ago in worship, our bell choir was performing "You raise me up," composed by Rolf Løvland and Brendan Graham. I began to think of the wonderment and beauty that was unfolding before me. I was totally present in the moment as I focused on the magnificent music. This miracle of music created a moment of reality that I couldn't express in words, it could only be experienced. I was "a cloud floating above a sea of peacefulness."

A cloud floating above a sea of peacefulness? Clearly, I was not a cloud. Further, what is a sea of peacefulness? I know what peacefulness is. But what is a sea of peacefulness? A sea is a vast body of water, sometimes anything

1. Dever, *What Did the Biblical Writers Know*, 122.

but peaceful. Yet, while I know that I was not a cloud floating above a sea of peacefulness, the statement is as true as the fact that I am now sitting on my front porch writing this sentence. More often than not direct literal description proves inadequate, and we can only explain moments of divine presence through metaphor and allegory. The arts, i.e., poetry, music, painting, and other forms, can express moments of reality unreachable by definitive description. In short, our subjective interiors cannot be adequately expressed by objective exterior explanations. Likewise, our response and experience of the divine can only be expressed indirectly as in metaphor.

This was the problem faced by biblical authors. How does one objectively express experiences of the divine? For example, how could one describe this man Jesus? Clearly his presence touched people beyond what could be definitively expressed. In his presence I felt as "a cloud floating above a sea of peacefulness." Perhaps that is how I would have written it. But, I was not there. Instead, Luke 2:13–14 says about his birth that "suddenly there was with the angel a multitude of the heavenly host, praising God and saying, 'Glory to God in the highest heaven, and on earth peace among those whom he favors!'" And so, we must not do damage to the Scriptures by reading them factually and literally. By identifying and understanding the many metaphorical examples we can begin to truly understand the magnificence of the man they called Jesus during his life, and the living Christ after his death.

God Doesn't Joke Around

I have a pretty good sense of humor and often invoke it spontaneously without much thought. In fact, I have used humor to make points with colleagues as well as to diffuse tense situations. But when we take the Scriptures as the literal word of God do we expect to find humor? Or do we put on a serious face and take it all too soberly? God doesn't joke around, or does (s)he? Maybe my spontaneous humor is God's gift to me that has gotten me through some rough patches. Perhaps even the Scriptures, being the biblical author's experience of the divine, have humor that we completely overlook. A problem with humor is that you have to know the context. If you have ever tried to tell a joke across cultures, you will know what I mean. Often the recipient of the humor doesn't get it. They lack the context and miss it. Trying to express humor not only across cultures, but also across two thousand years has some peculiar challenges. Nonetheless I suspect some of the Bible does contain humor which goes right over our heads when we only read it soberly and try to make literal sense of it.

An example of the spoofing occurs in John 4:7–15, as we have seen, with the interchanges between Jesus and the woman at the well. Jesus meets the Samaritan women at a well and asks for a drink of water, she hesitates and he says, "If you knew the gift of God, and who it is that is saying to you, 'Give me a drink,' you would have asked him, and he would have given you living water." Completely missing the point, she says, "Sir, you have nothing to draw with and the well is deep." In John 3:7 Jesus tells Nicodemus he must be born from above and Nicodemus thinks he had to go back into his mother's womb. This spoofing occurs on at least two levels. The first level pokes fun at the characters for their denseness. Both the woman and Nicodemus miss the point and appear rather foolish to the reader of these episodes. On the second level the spoofing is aimed at literalism in general. This is evident from the multiple occurrences of misinterpreted literalism that occur in John. I think John's writers are making the point that the mystery of divinity cannot be experienced through shallow rote understanding. Rather, one must dig deeper into reality. The Gospel of John uses spoofing to illustrate this.

There certainly had to be humor involved in Mark's telling of the story of Jesus healing the Gerasene Demonic in Mark 5:1–20. This heavily metaphoric story using labels such as Legion for the demons, an obvious reference to the Roman Legions, sending the demons into pigs, the mascot of Rome's tenth Legion occupying the region, and having the pigs run into the sea in the presence of divinity are not without their comedic elements. Maybe God does joke around after all, it is just done through you, me, a few biblical authors, and a host of others.

Three Steps Forward, Two Steps Backward: Creeping Culture

There are certainly confusing and conflicting parts of the Scriptures, as we have seen. This can be caused not only by literalizing the Bible's metaphors, but also by culture creeping in to water down some of Scripture's more radical propositions. For example, Borg and Crossan trace the radical vision of releasing slaves in Philemon to a less radical vision in Eph 6:5–9 where slaves are to obey their masters and masters are to treat their slaves kindly, to Titus 2:9–10 which doesn't even mention a master's responsibilities but says only, "Tell slaves to be submissive to their masters and to give satisfaction in every respect; they are not to talk back, not to pilfer, but to show complete and perfect fidelity." As indicated earlier, many believe that the latter two references attributed to Paul were not actually written by Paul. Nonetheless, this complete change of tenor from Philemon to Titus illustrates a demonstrable shift from a radical vision of God to an accommodation of human and cultural normalcy—a watering down of God's vision in order to accommodate the status quo.[2]

Fr. Richard Rohr has commented,

> Life itself—and Scripture too—is invariably three steps forward and two steps backward. It gets the point and then loses it or doubts it. In that, the biblical text mirrors our own human consciousness and journey. Our job is to see where the 'three steps forward' texts are heading (invariably toward mercy, forgiveness, inclusion, nonviolence, and trust), which then gives us the ability to recognize and guard against the 'two steps backward' texts (which are usually about vengeance on enemies, supposed divine wrath, law over grace, forms over substance, and technique over relationship).[3]

Here, Rohr speaks of the Bible as mirroring our human experience of moving ahead boldly and then losing ground. To do this requires more than a literal reading and a shallow and narrow interpretation. It requires a mature faith, one that leads us into a more holistic understanding of the human side of Scripture. Anything short of that leads one to look for proof texts to support preconceived views and opinions and to a far higher evaluation of one's own faith journey than is warranted.

If Borg, Crossan, and Rohr are correct, which I believe they are, then the Bible contains both God's vision for humanity as well as humanity's watering down of that vision. That is why both slavery advocates and abolitionists could turn to the Bible to support their respective cases. It is why we must never take concrete scriptural passages and apply them unthinkingly to today's issues and problems. Further, we must be careful to fully honor God's radical vision for humanity and not elevate the subversion of that vision to holiness just because it appears in the Bible.

2. Borg and Crossan, *First Paul*, 31–47.

3. Rohr, *Things Hidden*, 12.

Sorting Out the Mess

What are we to do? To start with, let's agree that taking the Bible literally is not a productive path. So let's write off this approach. As one commentator has said, "I can't believe anyone who thinks the Bible is the literal word of God has ever read it!" For example, it is easy for the literalist to follow the guidance of Deut 22:10 and not hitch an ox to a donkey to plow their field. I can only view this command in light of what we discussed earlier about humor in Scripture. Surely, the biblical author jests. However, let those who insist on literalism take their neighbor who gathers fire wood on the Sabbath to the city's edge and stone them to death as commanded in Num 15:32–36 or give like treatment to their rebellious son as commanded in Deut 21:18–21.

Secondly, when reading Scripture, look for the overriding moral issues it may be addressing. That is, consider the big picture message rather than the detail that can shift us back to literalism. Instead of fretting whether the healing stories of Jesus are real or mythical, focus on the bigger message that illness and deformity are not punishments from God, and the children of God should not shun the afflicted, but rather heal them.

Third, let's try to understand the context in which the Scriptures were written. We have heard so many times Paul's statement that in Christ there is no longer Jew or Gentile, male or female, slave or free. And to us it makes perfect sense. But how radical of an idea was this in the first century Greco-Roman culture? As we asked in chapter 2, what would Paul write today to break down the boundaries that separate and divide us? There are several good sources for understanding both ancient Israel and first century Greco-Roman culture such as William Dever's *What Did the Biblical Writers Know and When Did They Know It*, Rodney Stark's *The Rise of Christianity*, Scott Korb's *Life in Year One*, Crossan and Reed's *Excavating Jesus*, and Horsley and Hanson's *Bandits, Prophets, and Messiahs*. These and other references can be found in the bibliography.

Fourth, let's develop the skill of understanding metaphor. How many times have we been trying to figure out how Jesus could have fed the five thousand with five loaves and two fishes, as described in Matt 14:15–21? I have heard, as I am sure you have, every type of explanation as to how this could have happened: (1) it was a miracle; (2) people had their own lunch bag and when they shared there was more than enough for everyone; (3) it is merely a story made up to convince people of Jesus's divinity; (4) there was a McDonald's just a short piece down the road. Well perhaps I hadn't heard the last one. Think for a moment, couldn't the bread and fishes be the word and wisdom of Jesus? It was so rich that people could not digest all of it—it was more than they could consume.

Fifth, we must attempt to understand what the biblical author is trying to accomplish. For example, beyond the metaphorical understanding of the feeding miracle there was another objective. It was to make the case that Jesus was the one Moses spoke of in Deut 18. The parallel to Moses's feeding miracle in Exod 16:13–16 would not go unnoticed among Jewish audiences. Not only did Jesus feed the crowd with barely anything, but the crowd numbered five thousand. Similarly, while Moses parted the sea in the escape from Egypt, Jesus walked on the water and calmed the storm in the Gospels of Matthew, Mark, and John. Jesus was the prophet Moses spoke about, but not just like Moses, he was even more.

Finally, let's take continuing religious education seriously. Contemporary theologians and biblical scholars have produced many fine books and study materials for individual and group study. Continuing religious education will not answer the mysteries of God and reality, but it can help us mature in our faith. We should avoid attempts to define God or put God in a conveniently defined box. Perhaps in the tradition of apophatic theology, i.e., negative theology, we can get a better understanding of God by considering what God isn't. Continuing to ask questions and allowing your doubts to bubble to the surface will lead you to an ever more satisfactory understanding of God and reality. As it has been said, faith is a journey. The journey should require a more sophisticated understanding of Scripture than what literalism and fundamentalism can provide. Put on your hiking boots and continue along the trail.

In concluding his book Dever writes, "In reading the Bible, as with all great literature, one must see beyond the words, which are, after all, merely imperfect symbols, so the deeper reality of the author's vision of life [can be revealed]. That is the level at which the real 'meaning' of the text begins to appear, and to grasp it, one must read with empathy, intuition, imagination—and, may I say, with the spirit as well as with the mind."[4] Good advice!

---

4. Dever, *What Did the Biblical Writers Know*, 283.

8

God

Once Jesus was asked by the Pharisees when the kingdom of God was coming, and he answered, "The kingdom of God is not coming with things that can be observed; nor will they say, 'Look, here it is!' or 'There it is!' For, in fact, the kingdom of God is among you."

LUKE 17:20-21

The Great Beyond in Our Midst

IN CHAPTER 4 WE discussed Howard Thurman's comment that he wanted to write about Jesus as a religious subject and not a religious object. A short time ago I mentioned this in a study group and asked the difference between a subject and an object. One insightful person said an object is something you take down from the shelf and dust off occasionally. I thought that adequately described how we often treat God. We bring God off the shelf to dust off and use at our convenience.

Dietrich Bonhoeffer has argued that we keep God at the boundaries of our lives, calling upon God only when we are at the limits of our own abilities. In other words, putting God on a shelf to be dusted off and used when we get ourselves in a pickle. Bonhoeffer argued that God should be at the center of our lives as the "great beyond in our midst."[1] It was Jesus who said in Mark 12:27 that God is the God of the living, and in Luke 17:21 that the kingdom is among us. And that is where God is, in the midst of our

1. Bonhoeffer, *Letters and Papers*, 282.

being as the foundation of all that exists—not as an object we pull out and dust off when we reach the limit of our own resources.

In the Beginning

We really don't know much about the beginning. But we do know some things, though not with complete certainty, about the Christian tradition and its parenting that began with our Jewish forbearers. This takes us back prior to the formation of Israel in the early Iron Age around the thirteenth century BCE. During this period the Canaanite city-states were under the hegemony of the predominant military power of Egypt. But it was less than a unified effort, with frequent conflict between cities and general governing disarray. It was during this time that people began migrating out of the Canaanite cities and into the surrounding hill country west of the Jordan River. There they built and lived in small family compounds. Because of the terrain and climate, the people that Dever calls the Proto-Israelites practiced terrace farming and learned to capture rainwater in cisterns to counter the long periods of limited rainfall.

These Proto-Israelites initially brought with them the Canaanite gods. Dever puts it this way, "The more we learn about the official religion and especially about popular or folk religion in the entire biblical period, the more we see it is an outgrowth of Canaanite religion, no matter how much Yahwism eventually transformed it in the Monarchy."[2] The chief Canaanite God was El, the god of justice and compassion. Baal was the God of war and Asherah was the Mother God. Subsequently, it is believed a group coming from the Transjordan area south and east of the hill country brought a God of war known as Yahweh with many of the characteristics of Baal.[3] After a period of time Yahweh replaced Baal in their panel of gods. Some have argued that the group bringing Yahweh was the Exodus group who left Egypt with Moses; others disagree and believe the Exodus story to be a founding myth for the later kingdom of Israel.

Regardless, Yahweh became the supreme or at least official God of the Proto-Israelites, co-opting characteristics of El and to some extent Asherah to add to its similarities with Baal. As time advanced the kingdom of Israel was formed and Solomon in the mid-tenth century BCE constructed the First Temple and established the Temple Cult. About this time, priestly

2. Dever, *Who Were the Early Israelites*, 199–200.

3. Hiebert, *The Yahwist's Landscape*, 73.

authorities made the worship of other Canaanite gods verboten and Yahweh emerged as the God of Israel. This co-opting of El's and Asherah's qualities into Yahweh explains some of the confusing parts of the Old Testament Scriptures as the character of God assumed many seemingly contradictory characteristics, i.e., god of war, god of wisdom, god of compassion, as we have previously noted. But it even goes further than the Old Testament. These conflicting concepts are also the foundation for confusion surrounding two Christian understandings of God. They are: (1) the God of substitutionary atonement, believed by many, that requires the brutal death of Jesus as appeasement for an angry God; and (2) the God of love and compassion that inspires Jesus to tell us to forgive one another and even love those who persecute us. So, if you are confused about all of these seemingly conflicting views of God, you at least know how some of it came about.

Beyond Anthropomorphism?

The difficulty in resolving the contradictory Scriptures about God, especially in the Old Testament, is found in one's understanding of Scripture. We have addressed this before, but it bears repeating here. If one assumes that the Bible is the literal word of God, as though it is a transmission directly from the divine, then we have a very confusing situation. On the other hand, if we understand the Scriptures to be human's reaching out in efforts to understand the divine and their expression of the divine living within and among them, at different times, in different cultures, and with different levels of knowledge, we can understand how the expressions and experiences could be quite different. We cannot escape the fog of culture, incomplete knowledge, and human imperfection when we ascribe meaning to our experiences, including that of divinity. As the Apostle Paul so aptly put it in 1 Cor 13:12a, "For now we see in a mirror, dimly. . . . " It was true prior to Paul, it was true for Paul, and it is true today.

It is difficult for us to conceive of God as anything other than a supernatural being. The word God itself is a human construct. As such, to illustrate the divinity of God beyond human capacity it is only natural to ascribe titles such as the Almighty, Lord, or Sovereign. We talk to God in prayer, we refer to God as Father, and we naturally assign God superhuman qualities. Some think of God as omnipotent, able to whimsically do anything she pleases. Some believe that God could keep us from danger, and sometimes does, but at other times chooses not to do so. This thinking creates all kinds of theological problems. When one is not protected and calamity comes, is it because I am unworthy? Is God punishing me? Did I not pray enough or correctly? Is my faith insufficient? All of these reflections promote self-guilt and diminish one's personal sense of wellbeing. Perhaps we should consider another way of conceiving and experiencing the divine. Paul Tillich has argued that God is not a being at all. Rather, he argues that God is the ground of all being. God is that which makes all things exist. Paul Knitter adds that God can be thought of not only as the ground of all being, but also the ground of all becoming, i.e., the initiator of all that exists and all that will or can exist. From this perspective Knitter understands God as the connecting spiritual energy of reality. Perhaps this is what Luke meant when he wrote in Acts 17:27b–28, "Though indeed he is not far from each one of us. For in him we live and move and have our being."

We know that God lies beyond human comprehension and is shrouded in mystery. We know that all attempts to define God are futile. God is simply more than we can fit words and symbols around. This is the reason behind the metaphor, parable, and even hyperbole we find in Scripture and religious writing. Yet the human need for concreteness over the centuries has led to the assignment of certain qualities to God. Some of these emanate from contradictory Scripture mentioned earlier and others from apocryphal and legendary sources. How are we to sort through these often conflicting, confusing, and sometimes unbelievable qualities attributed to God? I believe an approach we introduced in the last chapter has some merit; that is, through a negation approach. The technical term for this is apophatic theology. It is an approach to understanding God by what you believe God is not. This may not seem very satisfying. However, by not prematurely foreclosing on your understanding, it is compatible with a growing and expanding understanding of the divine and dampens the proclivity of making your God too small and self-serving. It may even resist limiting God to our own religious tribe. Perhaps an example may help clarify this discussion. The image of God as father has been well received by many. However, it has not been well received by some Christians. Some reject this imagery because their own father may have been abusive toward them. Others may find the feminine expressions of God found in the Psalms and elsewhere more satisfying and inspirational. This has led some to substitute the word Creator or Mother/Father for Father in the Lord's Prayer. This is a way of using negative theology. The underlying principle here is that God does not have a gender or at least God is not male. With a negative approach one may not know precisely what God is, but they may firmly come to believe what God is not. In doing so they may eliminate some things attributed to God that may otherwise have been misleading and dysfunctional.

Walter Wink would argue that we cannot discard an anthropomorphic understanding of God. Indeed, while God is multidimensional, undefinable, and surrounded with mystery, a dimension of God is also fully human. Without that human dimension it would be impossible for humans to relate to the Godhead. By God being fully human we infer that we human beings have not yet evolved into full humanity. In our present state of development we still engender many inhumane qualities. It is the fully human qualities of God that were incarnate in Jesus of Nazareth and through which Jesus lived in God and God in Jesus. The English theologian, Austin Farrer, has said that Jesus was God's self-enacted parable.[4] That being said, and following Wink's lead, we can also take a positive approach to understanding the human qualities of God. But it is not through Jesus's death and resurrection. It is through Jesus's life as the actualization of his teaching that we can experience the essence of God's human qualities.

It is the life of Jesus that gives us the concrete knowledge of the human dimension of God. It is also this human part of God that resides in our depths, challenging us to ever-higher levels of humaneness and to a life of fullness in God. Some might choose to replace the term God with Deep Spirit. This conceptualization avoids limitations inherent in the more common independent super human construct of God and encompasses a life force that can illuminate and empower. This Deep Spirit is found not only at the core of the self, but also in our relationships with others and with our experiences with nature, art forms, and especially stillness.

Miracles

Regardless of how we think about the reality of God, whether it is as a super being, as the great beyond in our midst,s or as Deep Spirit and spiritual energy, how are we to live with this God? Perhaps a place to start is with thankfulness for the wonderment of miracles. We tend to think of miracles as being events that lie outside the laws of nature, i.e., supernatural events. But it is precisely the laws of nature that are the miracles. Look at the natural world about you. Its beauty is unfathomable. We think we have things figured out and so much of our daily encounters are predictable. But

4. Farrer, "Revelation," 98.

consider the wonder in the predictable. We become hungry and eat. We did not think of being hungry, it just happens. Then we eat and are satisfied. But that is not the end. The food is digested, converted into sugars which feed, repair, and energize our vast cellular system. Waste is carried off and eliminated. It works flawlessly in the healthy organism. And it all happens without any conscious or deliberate act on our part. A miracle indeed!

I recently had surgery to repair spinal deterioration that was causing an impingement on my sciatic nerve. The surgery was called "minimally invasive." I would have to say that this was obviously from the surgeon's perspective. Nonetheless, the miracle of advancing medical science and practice is astounding. But even more astounding is the healing process of the human body. Just consider the miracle of a physical entity repairing itself. Obviously, it doesn't always work, but most of the time it does. When it does, we must not just take it for granted, we need to recognize it for the miracle it is and praise our creator.

As another example, let's revisit the moment I sat in worship with the bell choir performing "You Raise Me Up." I said that it made me feel as a cloud floating above a sea of peacefulness. But let's consider the miracle that moment captured. There was the original miracle of turning an inspiration into melody and lyrics by the Secret Garden's Rolf Løvland and Brendan Graham. There was the concerted effort of twelve musicians and the director, all dedicated to performing the work. Beyond that, there was the extraction of ore from the earth, its refinement into brass, followed by the foundry work, and the fine craftsmanship that formed the bells. There was the complexity of the sanctuary in which we sat and all the efforts and materials that it took to form it. There was the physics of the sound waves that carried the vibration of the bells to my ears and amazing neurosensory cells that carried it to my brain to create the sensation of not just sound, but beautiful music. Then finally there was the complex associations stored in my mind that touched past experiences creating in me warmth and peace that truly surpassed all empirical description. If nothing else, this moment verified for me that the miracles of God were alive and well, still working in history, and I was like a cloud floating above a sea of peacefulness.

Our cognitive abilities are a true miracle. Our social structures that bring food to the table, the beauty of nature that regenerates our soul, the mystery of insight and innovative thinking, and the inspiration of music and poetry—they are all miraculous. Thanks be to God. Living with thankful and mindful wonderment of this miraculous reality in which we exist is perhaps a first step in putting God back into the conscious center of our lives as Dietrich Bonhoeffer would urge us.

Location, Location, Location

The ancients believed in a three-tiered universe. Above were the heavens and the home of God. On the earth was the place of mortals and below the underworld contained the shadowy realm of the dead. As our knowledge of the heavens increased through the science of astronomy, we placed God in some other domain, but still as a separate being, although of almighty proportion. As we noted, Dietrich Bonhoeffer described God as the great beyond in our midst. Paul Tillich argued that God is found deep within us and is not a being at all, but is rather the ground of all being, the foundation for all that exists. And Knitter has added that God is not just the ground of all being, but the ground of all becoming as well.

The problem seems to be in the way we too often visualize God. If we envision God as a superhuman being, a king if you will, with powers to do anything at any moment, then we need to plead for this God to come into our lives and save us. But if we understand God as the life force of all existence, like Paul Tillich has argued, then we don't need to call God from somewhere else to be with us and rescue us. Rather, God is always present. God can perhaps be thought of as the essence of reality, the glue that holds all things together and the empowering spirit that makes things happen. Consider God embedded in all that exists, in each of us and in all living and nonliving entities. If this is the case then God is not to be called from elsewhere. Rather, in our travail we must seek the divine living deep within us and the comfort of the divine living deep in the community of our human family.

The Jewish philosopher Emmanuel Levinas has written that there is a compelling unknowable draw or force in the other that commands us, and that we find our ground of being in this force. A person of a religious bent might call this force the divine. This is not unlike Knitter's notion of the divine as a unifying spiritual energy, which we discussed a bit earlier. Luke 7:20–21 says the essence of God is in our midst, which may alternatively be translated the essence of God is within us and therefore amongst all. Suppose, as Tillich and Knitter argue, that we find God in our depth and in that depth God is not a separate being, but rather that which makes our being and our becoming possible. In such a case it would then follow that the divine is to be found not only deep within each of us, but deep within every human being and all of creation. Tillich further argues that we rarely experience this depth, but instead busily entertain ourselves by rushing around on our surface. Perhaps this is not unlike the distinction that Richard Rohr makes between the false self and the true self. The false self is that self we create through our socialization and learning processes. It is the self we define autonomously, express to others, and too often use as a measuring stick for destructive self-criticism. The true self is the divine that lives within each of us and therefore among us. It is often the false self that dominates our existence and we fail to be in touch with our true self. This true self is the depth, in Tillich's words, where we find God.

If the divine lives deep within each of us and is that force which may unite us and transcend our false self, it behooves us to break down the walls that separate us from one another. Remove that which defines us as self and other, and realize our true common humanity that lives and exists within that divinity we call God. In that process we honor our differences, but also hold in higher esteem our commonness. Further, an act that diminishes or destroys another human or somehow limits them from becoming all they are capable of becoming is an assault not just on the other, but it is a direct assault on all of us and on divinity itself—something we might truly call evil. Jesus spoke not just of a personal salvation, but also of community. He called it the kingdom of God. It is not a state of receiving divinity thorough some external process to become more fully human, but a process of personal striving drawing on the divinity from within to become ever more fully human. In this process a more fully human community, state, and global society can emerge and be nurtured.

This perspective has implications for our social pact within and between nations. It is a true prolife agenda. By prolife I do not mean to stray into the realm of antiabortion rhetoric, but rather to redirect our human and material resources to those institutions and practices that build humanity and create opportunities for all peoples to live a life of transcendence and value. This is a life not just for themselves, but for their brothers and sisters of every distinction, everywhere. There is no definitive uniqueness that overshadows our common divinity. Our task is to move past the ordinary and to be drawn to experience the divine in the depth of ourselves and others and thus worship not a distant God, but the one that lives within and among us all.

9

Church

Henceforth the world will be able to make the sign of the cross only with a cross that has become a symbol of growth at the same time as of redemption.

PIERRE TEILHARD DE CHARDIN

CENTURIES HAVE PASSED SINCE Jesus walked the pathways of ancient Palestine. Our understanding of the world about us has changed dramatically. Our knowledge grew slowly at first, but with our breakthroughs in thought and technology our acquisition of knowledge accelerated. We reached a stage in the mid-twentieth century and perhaps earlier when it began to grow exponentially. Along the way many of our superstitions were discredited and our worldviews shattered. We no longer believe in a three-tiered universe of the ancients, with God above and the evil one below. We no longer believe that the sun orbits the earth. Demons are no longer thought to cause disease. We are even beginning to rethink our concept of God not as a being, but as the ground of being and all becoming; the foundation for all that exists and can exist. Not only has our world matured and our knowledge expanded, but also the tools and methods of investigation have advanced. We not only know more, we have an enhanced capacity to expand our knowledge and make ever more precise measurements and observations. With our large knowledge platform and sophisticated methodologies we can now have an even more comprehensive knowledge about the historical past than people who actually lived in the past.

Within all these dynamics, how has the church fared? Some churches have changed. Many churches have now gravitated to a contemporary format in which the music is modern, liturgy is minimized, and technology and social media are ubiquitous. These contemporary churches make attendance convenient with ample parking, parking attendants, and easy in and out. Still other churches have remained traditional. Their services relatively unchanged for decades with some minor innovations such as bell choirs or offering an additional contemporary style of service. Still others seek a more progressive stance within the traditional framework, addressing cultural issues and promoting inclusiveness and tolerance. But is this enough? Or, with our expanded knowledge, should the church be rethinking its fundamental message? Should the meaning of the Jesus story be recast and rethought just as it has throughout the history of the church as new ways of engaging the people became necessary in a changing and maturing culture? Is it the way the story as now told that is responsible for the decline in church affiliation and the rapid rise in the unaffiliated? Has the church failed to play a meaningful role as a critic of society beyond participation in the culture wars of abortion and homosexuality? Has religion and nationalism become too closely aligned? Have we not yet shaken off the co-opting of the church by empire that occurred early in the fourth century under Constantine? Do clergy feel restrained from sharing with their congregants the contemporary biblical scholarship and twenty-first-century theology that they studied in all but the most conservative seminaries? Is it too inconvenient for clergy to challenge people to think deeper and more honestly? And where are the congregants in all of this? Are they still stuck with a faith they learned in childhood and do not wish to grow beyond? Was Brian McLaren correct when he wrote, "The only way Christianity can become salvageable is by admitting that it is unsalvageable in its present form"?[1] Finally, does the church elevate tradition above truth, comfort above challenge, and safety above sacrifice? If any of this rings true, what should be done about it? These are issues we will address in this final chapter.

Back to the Bathwater

In chapter 4, there is a section entitled "Jesus and the Bathwater." It introduced the idea that some doctrines have outlived their time and should be

1. McLaren, *Great Spiritual Migration*, 75.

abandoned without throwing out Jesus in the process. In this section we are going to again briefly address penal substitutionary atonement, which forms a core message for many churches, both contemporary and traditional. This concept was the topic of chapter 5. You will easily recognize it. It goes like this: (1) we have fallen from perfection into sinfulness; (2) we are helpless and unable to lift ourselves out of sinfulness; (3) God is incapable of forgiving us without some type of compensation; (4) no ordinary compensation would appease God's anger with us; (5) God sent his only son to brutally die on a cross as the perfect sacrificial compensation; and (6) this sacrifice appeased God once and for all and God is reconciled with all who confess Jesus as their Lord and Savior, and will give them eternal life.

Penal substitutionary atonement has its roots in the cultic sacrificial and scapegoating practices of the ancient world as depicted in chapter 5. Paul and other New Testament writers metaphorically drew upon these practices to explain the saving power of Jesus's crucifixion and resurrection. It is based on the fall from grace recounted in the Garden of Eden story (Gen 3) from which Augustine developed his early fifth-century doctrine of original sin. Also part of this narrative is an offended God that needed a retributive sacrifice in order to forgive humanity for their depravity. Since humans could not provide a significant enough sacrifice, God substituted his own unblemished and perfect son, Jesus, as the sacrifice. All the sins of the world were placed on Jesus as the scapegoat for our sinful nature and thus he was sacrificed in our place.

Atonement theology is endemic in today's Christianity. There is rarely a worship service in which "Jesus died for my sins" is not explicitly or implicitly called upon. Hymns with themes of blood sacrifice and blood purification are sung each Sunday in many of our contemporary churches. Yet think of what this thematically implies about God. It implies that God does not have the capacity to forgive. Didn't Jesus admonish us not to hold grudges, to love our enemies and pray for those who persecute us? Didn't Jesus forgive sins and teach others they could forgive sins before he was put to death on the cross? But under substitutionary atonement, God must have his pound of flesh, in this case the torture and crucifixion of Jesus. This is nothing more than a disturbing compensatory exchange model. How could such a construct be a fundamental characteristic of God? Is this a god that cannot forgive without payback? Is this the god we wish to emulate and worship?

Early in the second century CE the early church father Irenaeus wrote about God having a long-term plan for the perfection of the imperfect human. He believed that over time mankind would evolve into becoming fully human. A key intervention in this evolutionary process was the incarnated Jesus who, in the words of the theologian Austin Farrer, was God's self-enacted parable. Jesus was the perfectly evolved, fully human model for mankind emulate. About eighteen centuries later, Pierre Teilhard de Chardin, the French philosopher, paleontologist, and (frequently censured) Jesuit priest drawing on this theological background and his scientific training proposed that a fall from grace (as suggested by the Garden of Eden myth) never occurred. He proposed that rather than instantaneous creation, God creates in an evolutionary manner, bringing together diverse elements to create new, albeit initially imperfect, entities that improve over time. From matter evolved primitive life, then higher forms of life, and to this point human beings with the capacity for consciousness. In that creative process of bringing together diverse elements into new wholeness there are imperfections which explain the presence of evil or sin, i.e., missing the mark. In Teilhard de Chardin's theology the redemptive act of Jesus is not to appease an angry God, but rather God's act to demonstrate the perfection into which humans can evolve. In this sense, very much in line with the Gospel of John, Jesus represents or is the embodiment of the eternal logos or plan or vision for humanity that has not yet fully evolved, except perhaps in a few pockets or incidents of history. Teilhard de Chardin's call was to adjust Christian theology such that science and religion were two sides of the same coin rather than divergent paths conflicting and competing with one another. He wrote,

> At this very moment we have reached a delicate point of balance at which a readjustment is essential. It could not, in fact, be otherwise: our Christology is still expressed in exactly the same terms as those which, three centuries ago, could satisfy men whose outlook on the cosmos it is now physically impossible for us to accept.[2]

While published after his death, Teilhard de Chardin wrote this in 1933. It is as valid today as it was to him when he wrote it over eighty years ago.

John Shelby Spong argues that traditional Christianity is based on a wrongful analysis of human nature. He also doesn't think we have fallen from perfection into sin.[3] From the very beginning of life it has been evolving into higher forms of consciousness. From early single-celled organisms

---

2. Teilhard de Chardin, *Christianity and Evolution*, 77.

3. Spong, *Biblical Literalism*, 203–9.

to early plant and animal species, through ever more sophisticated life forms, humans evolved. Along the way unconsciousness grew into primitive consciousness, into more advanced consciousness and finally into our stage of self-consciousness. Contrary to falling from perfection into sin, humans have evolved into the highest common level of consciousness yet achieved. It is the story of progression, not regression. But is it over? Is there more to come? Is there the possibility of evolving from our current self-absorbed preoccupation with survival into a Jesus-like divinity as Irenaeus suggested 1,800 years ago? Could it be that Jesus was the breakthrough person, the one to have evolved into this state and is the standard bearer for our next higher stage of consciousness? Could it be that we today are actually proto-Christians, with the potential to evolve into full Christ-like divine human beings?

Suppose we entertain Teilhard de Chardin's and Spong's analysis for a moment. What might that mean? First, humans not falling from grace, but rather evolving into perfection suggests that what we need from our theology is not an assertion that we are in a constant state of sin and therefore guilt, but empowerment to grow into our created potential. Spong believes that our theology needs to empower us to become all that we are capable of becoming. We have already evolved into a high level of self-consciousness, but can we evolve into a state of universal consciousness whereby we shun our dualisms and celebrate our common nature. A God of love and compassion that works through and in spite of our imperfection to empower us to transcend our egocentric stage of development is indeed a God that is to be worshiped and emulated.

Consider what lies ahead for us if humans could evolve into a Jesus-like divinity. Would we not feel obligated to end greed and ensure adequate life resources for all people? Would we not perfect our diplomacy skills and end war as a solution to our problems? Would we not respect the human dignity of all of our brothers and sisters? Would not justice roll down like waters, and righteousness like an ever-flowing stream as Amos wrote so many centuries ago? Is this not what God has been pulling us toward for millennia with Jesus being the ultimate forbearer of what our next stage would be?

Over the centuries some have either achieved this state or at least approached it. A number have been called apostles and still others saints. They moved beyond being consumed by their own self-interest to endorse more universal concerns, often giving their lives in return. While humanity in general has not developed to this stage, does this way of understanding God and

Jesus not give us a greater hope for the future than a theology laden with guilt from a mythical fall in the Garden of Eden from which only the brutal death of Jesus could atone? Does this not seem a more appropriate way to tell the human story and our relationship with the divine? You may pause to ask, is this biblical? I believe many literalists may say no! But in my view a mature understanding of the teaching of Jesus leads to an enthusiastic yes! As we have seen, taking the Bible literally more often than not misses the point. Further, it requires us to put aside at least two thousand years of accumulated knowledge that was not available to the ancients. We use that knowledge everyday of our lives, except perhaps for an hour or two on Sunday morning. A faith with integrity obliges us to bring our full selves to worship, not just our bodies and perhaps half our intellect. I don't know if Spong's scenario is the path we should pursue. Possibly we should leave it to teams of theologians and biblical scholars to further flesh out a twenty-first-century understanding of the Jesus narrative. Walter Wink's groundbreaking scholarship outlined in his book *The Human Being* is a clear example of this initiative. What I am convinced of is that we cannot continue to use worn out doctrines that make little sense in light of all we have learned and still expect our churches to survive. No, Jesus did not suffer and die on the cross to appease an angry God because of our sinfulness and fall from grace. He died to show us how to transcend our fear and self-centeredness to evolve into a more fully human stage of universal development.

The Case for an Immoral Church

Robin Meyers writes about Jesus being a corrupting influence in the Roman Empire.[4] He took this thought from the parable of the yeast (Luke 13:20–21), where a woman mixes yeast into a large quantity of flour until it is all leavened. Dr. Meyers explains that in the first century the word translated as leaven meant corruption. In this sense, the kingdom of God is a corrupting force challenging the accepted cultural norms and practices of the time. His point is that corruption of the empire is what the church should be about today. Rather than acquiescing to the culture and empires of our day, the church should nonviolently challenge and speak out against the injustice that accompanies concentrated power and unchecked economic greed. This is the task of the immoral church. But what does immorality have to do with this?

4. Meyers, *Underground Church*, 166–91.

I am not using the term immoral in the sense of depravity or wicked-ness. Rather I am picking up on Gordon Kaufman's conceptualization of morality.[5] In his book, *In Face of Mystery*, Kaufman states that individuals have three basic commandments. They are to act, to act morally, and to act ethically. It works this way. As human beings we differ from all other living entities. Plant life has quite limited mobility and options for survival. While it is true that some plants have developed an amazing facility to adapt to their environment, generally, if there is not suitable soil with sustainable moisture the plant will not survive. Animals have more freedom in that they are mobile and can seek sustenance and safety through a number of simple to sophisticated, yet mostly instinctual behaviors. But like plants, the animal kingdom is primarily limited by its genetics.

Humans have much greater capacity for self-definition and self-deter-mination. Indeed, they can not only develop more sophisticated strategies for obtaining sustenance and safety, but they can aspire to higher level needs such as love and self-actualization. Humans can transcend their genetics to not only escape unpleasant or threatening environments, but can actually change their environment to avoid future threats to survival. They can till the ground and plant seed to raise crops and stabilize their food supply. They can dam rivers and streams to create reservoirs to offset drought. They can cooperate, creating institutions for common defense, education, and healing the infirm. This gift of self-determination places an obligation on humans to act and not merely be passive travelers through time and space.

Kaufman further says we should act morally. Over time cultures and societies develop a set of right attitudes and acceptable behaviors. These attitudes and behaviors are the values that support and maintain the com-munity and promote cohesion. Shared values give the community function-ality, common purpose, and shared responsibilities. Kaufman argues that we should act within the moral framework of values and accepted practices of our communities to preserve and strengthen unity and effectiveness.

But one should also act ethically. In common usage moral and ethical behavior are often indistinguishable. However, Kaufman makes the follow-ing distinction. While morality pertains to the set of values and practices a community has developed over time, ethics pertains to the critique of those values and practices. Ethical inquiry assesses the consistency of mor-al behaviors and attitudes with respect to higher principled values. While morality looks backward on what has been decided in the past, ethics looks

5. Kaufman, *In Face of Mystery*, 202–9.

forward considering how tomorrow's community can be more compassionate and just. For example, racial segregation was part of the moral code in the southern United States from after the Emancipation Proclamation of 1862 ended slavery until the Civil Rights Act of 1964. The ethical critique and subsequent civil unrest of the 1950s and 1960s ended the legality and acceptability of racial segregation. As evidenced by this account, ethical critique is, often as not, accompanied by societal upheaval. Outdated morals die a difficult death.

Too often conservative Christianity has been on the wrong side of history. It has sought to maintain the social fabric rather than critique it, often drawing on Scripture for support. For example, it resisted the civil rights movement, eschewed women's rights (some churches still exclude woman from its leadership), and some even clamored for war in Afghanistan and Iraq. Churches in the nineteenth and early twenty centuries used the Bible to justify slavery and oppose women's suffrage. And now many churches use ancient biblical verses to oppose accepting our LGBTQ brothers and sisters into full ecclesial participation. Far too many traditional churches stay on the sidelines taking no position at all, failing to take on even Kaufman's most basic commandment to act, thinking it is the moral thing to do. I believe it is time for the church to rise up and distance itself from the dysfunctional aspects of our common culture—especially those aspects of culture that promote violence, overpower compassion, and thwart justice. No one country, society, or clique contains God's preferred children. All people are equally loved by God. It is time for the church to represent only God's community which has no borders or boundaries. The church should stand beyond the contemporary moral fabric of nation and culture, proclaiming peace and justice for all and calling into question all norms, practices, and customs that dehumanize or diminish the dignity of any person or group, anywhere. That is the case for the immoral church.

Courage in the Pulpit/Open-Mindedness in the Pew

In her controversial book, *With or Without God*, Gretta Vosper wrote, "A silent pact often exists between pastor and congregation, a pact in which certain difficult issues are to be left unmentioned. . . . As long as laity don't have to think about it pastors don't have to talk about it. As long as pastors don't talk about it, the laity don't think about it."[6]

6. Vosper, *With or Without God*, 44–45.

It is becoming common knowledge that clergy have learned things in seminary that they never preach from the pulpit. They keep much of contemporary biblical scholarship to themselves. Why? Perhaps it is easier to go along with what most people already believe. Why rock the boat? After all, being a pastor is a career and sometimes a precarious one at that. Who wants to ruin their career and livelihood by introducing ideas that will not be well received? Many pastors have families to support and losing their position would create a hardship. Besides, preaching is only a part of the job. There are also the administrative and pastoral functions which consume inordinate amounts of time and energy. Why should a pastor jeopardize her position with new and possibly troubling proposals about faith? It is often safer to use ambiguous wording, soft literalism, and other techniques that leave passive listeners believing that their pastor believes just as they do. But will these practices foster a deeper spiritual yearning and mature faith among the flock? Of course not! It can only perpetuate the decline in Christianity that we see occurring today. Where is the courage in the pulpit?

On the other hand, why is intellectual curiosity, open-mindedness, and a yearning for deeper spiritual understanding mostly absent in the pew? Why are so many congregants satisfied with not going beyond the religious training they received as children? Again I ask, why do so many live all week long using their best intellect only to abandon it when they sit in the pew or attend an adult Sunday school class? Anyone attending adult Bible classes should be appalled when they are confronted with over simplicity and mediocre instruction. But typically we either sit in silence or vote with our feet, i.e., avoid attending them. Euphemistically speaking, is this any way to run a railroad? Why isn't more demanded?

And so I ask and challenge, where is the courage in the pulpit and the open-mindedness and yearning for a deeper spiritual understanding in the pew? I believe that for Christianity to survive in this millennium we need a sea change from where we are today in our evangelical and mainline churches to a more intellectually and spiritually fulfilling church experience.

Christian Renewal

The town of Divide, Colorado, where I live, lies in the Rocky Mountains at 9,200 feet above sea level. As such, spring arrives late. It is estimated that spring arrives one day later for every hundred feet of altitude. That adds up to about four more months of winter for Divide residents than most people in the United States experience. But winter in the Rockies is not all that bad. While long and very cold at times, we also get over three hundred days of sunshine. Subsiding winter storms are followed by the purest blue skies imaginable. The sun heats the earth and its inhabitants with unimaginable warmth even when the thermometer records freezing temperatures. This year we have had ample moisture and we look forward to a bumper crop of wildflowers which will prolifically cover the open fields.

Everywhere has its own variety of beauty. What is amazing is how life regenerates itself after even the harshest of winters. I no longer see myself in the spring of life's cycle. Yet I can feel that way each spring season. It is a sense of renewal and an opportunity to take stock of my situation. I have found that while that happens each year, there is also a sabbatical rebirth that occurs when I must think seriously about where I have been in life and what direction my life should take in the future. Some have called this the seven-year itch. The ancient Hebrews knew about this wisdom and set free its slaves and cancelled debts during the sabbatical year, providing a release of burden and an opportunity for a new beginning. Things that continue without renewal and rethinking become stagnant and in the stages of a death grip. The same could be said about the church. Is it time to rethink church? I believe it is.

Rethink Message

It is time to rethink the message of the church. Often the message has been drenched in dualism. You must believe this to be in; else you are part of the out. There needs to a move toward greater inclusiveness. This is not the early fourth century when we had to decide what beliefs Christians must have to be orthodox. Many churches struggle with inclusiveness and some have had limited success. One denomination has the motto "Open Minds, Open Hearts, Open Doors." That is a good start, but it has been difficult to implement. Other churches remain stodgily stuck in their exclusive ways, unabashedly thinking they have knowledge beyond what any human could possibly know. The church also needs to foster dialogue across religious divisions that can expand our knowledge of how others understand and experience divinity and thus enhance our own understanding. In that process we will increase our tolerances for other world religions and reduce our own tendency toward inwardness and exclusivity. As Newell has observed, "The historic religions of the world are given not to compete with each other but to complete each other."[7] Let's be open to God speaking to us whatever the source.

We need to reform our theology and move from a sin/guilt model to an empowerment model. Jesus died for my sins is no longer a viable theology for the twenty-first century or any century going forward. As we rapidly expand our knowledge in all areas from the days of antiquity to today's inquiry into the basic building blocks of matter and energy, we need a concept of God that does justice to our intellect. As we understand matter and energy to be interchangeable and light to sometimes behave like waves and other times like particles, we need to eschew artificial dualisms in our thinking. We need a theology that brings us universalism and diminishes particularism. We need a theology of hope rather than hopelessness—not one based on some life beyond life, or on an end time apocalypse, but one based on a life of meaning, spiritual wellbeing, and connectedness, one that stresses grace and forgiveness of self and others, one that honors all of God's children and demonizes none of them. This theology makes Jesus not a victim, but rather a vision of what we all can evolve into.

We need to rethink our Christian foundations moving from doctrine to faith. We need to expand understanding and not promulgate statements of belief. We need to comprehend Jesus's message and internalize it. We do not need to overemphasize beliefs about the nature of his divinity, rather we should focus more on the practices endemic in his divinity. Emulation is the highest form of worship. It is like the old story of the pig and the chicken with respect to ham and eggs. The chicken is involved, perhaps at a level similar to us when we attend a worship service. But the pig is committed, putting his all into the ham. We must be like the pig if we seek to evolve into the universal consciousness of Jesus.

Rethink Church and Society

Some denominations are involved in contemporary society. They play a positive role in their communities with food banks, shelters, involvement in nonprofit organizations, and similar activities. These are all good things. But the church needs to have a stronger voice in promoting justice and caring for the orphan, widow, and alien. The church needs a stronger voice in how we set our national priorities, how we pursue peace versus war, and how we live our values as a nation both at home and abroad. The church

7. Newell, *Rebirthing of God*, 43.

needs to be critical of society standing beyond it and not act as its accomplice. It does not need to promote one political party over another as some churches have done. But the church needs to be political and hold both parties accountable to the time honored Judeo Christian values we hold sacrosanct and as such be the moral compass of our society.

Rethink Clergy/Lay Roles

I will say this as plainly as I can. We do not need to dumb down Christianity for it to be acceptable. Many clergy attend seminary and go on to advanced theological study. All of this is on top of a four-year undergraduate degree program. They have many roles to fulfill in the church. Educating the flock should not be among the least of them. Clergy must step up to the plate and honestly present Christianity with integrity. Congregants must encourage this and provide clergy supportive cover when they do so. Congregants need to open themselves to journey in faith. Being a Christian is not a one-time event. It is a continuing journey in which one meets the divine. We must break down the pact of clergy silence and congregant apathy.

Christ and Buddha

Thich Nhat Hahn writes, "We don't look for Buddha in his body; we look for Buddha in his teachings. The Buddha is continued through his teachings and practices. In this way we can be in touch with the Buddha in the present moment."[8] Being in touch with the divinity of the fully human Jesus, which to varying degrees lives in all of us, is being in solidarity with the essence and teachings of Jesus. He gave us the truth that saves us from ourselves and other such foolishness. Let us keep the resurrection of Jesus alive and bring truth and the insane sanity of God's wisdom back into the church and our lives in a thoughtful reformation and Christian renewal. Let us initiate this new beginning sooner, rather than later!

8. Hahn, *Peace of Mind*, 64.

Epilogue

TRADITIONAL CHRISTIANITY IS SLOWLY dying. Between 2007 and 2014 the number of adults identifying as Christian dropped precipitously. The declines fall across all age groups, but increases with each younger decade. All of the Mainline Protestant and Catholic congregations are declining as a portion of the population. The evangelical churches have also declined, except for the few nondenominational evangelicals which have shown modest growth.

The doctrines and creeds that served the church well for centuries are no longer viable for postmodern people. That is consistent with the moderate success of the nondenominational evangelicals which tend to minimize liturgy, creeds, and doctrine, yet still promulgate their message in creedal and doctrinal ways. Clergy have less influence as education and information becomes more widely available to the general population and the church fades as the social center for the family. The church in general seems to have withdrawn into issues of personal piety at the expense of providing leadership in advancing social issues.

All of this is probably most disturbing to older Mainline Protestants and Catholics who have been faithful to the church over the decades. But even some of them are abandoning the Christian ship. Spirituality is not dead; it is just being serviced outside the church. So where is this future taking the church and does the church still have a purpose? Can it again be the nurturer of spirituality? I think it can and it must. But it can't be the same old business as usual. The church is in need of an overhaul. We need to look at the successes of the nondenominational churches and their non-liturgical services. We need to begin to think differently about the nature of God and how we tell the Jesus story. We need to again become the moral compass of society, not from a pious vantage point, but from a communal one. The church needs to be political, but not partisan. It needs to be educational, not doctrinal. It needs to pump new ideas, new excitement, and new innovation into its tired mantra. It needs to holistically address adults as mature thinking human beings satisfying their intellect as well as their heart. It needs to empower people to emulate the breakthrough nature of Jesus, putting aside their particularism and embracing universalism. This book was designed to be a resource for such a new beginning.

In this book many of the problems and issues of Christianity in the twenty-first century have been revealed. Over the past several years I have read about needed reforms for Christianity. They are usually followed with prescriptions for how to resolve some of the difficulties identified. I am usually disappointed with their solutions. And that is part of the problem. They are often writing with the agenda to provide consulting solutions, sell copies of their books, or put a band-aid on deep cuts. That is not my objective. The solutions to the present problems of Christianity do not have shallow or self-serving answers. The solutions must be fundamental and wide sweeping. Christianity will survive or die based on the validity of the messages of Jesus that survive this modern age. If he is truly the logos as the Gospel of John proclaims, then Christianity will continue because it is the truth, the way, and the life. It just needs to present itself in the genre that speaks to the twenty-first-century mind-set. The solutions are to be found by you and the Great Spirit of Life. Not necessarily as a religion, but as a "way." Amen.

Appendix I

The Historical Backdrop and Politics of First-Century Galilee

Historical Events Leading Up to Jesus's Galilee

JESUS GREW FROM CHILDHOOD into adulthood in the small town of Nazareth, population of about four hundred, located in Lower Galilee. His birth was around the year 4 BCE, close to the time of the death of Herod the Great, King of the Jews, who ruled the region beginning in 37 BCE and lasting until his death. Galilee is located in the hill country of northern Israel. It lies to the north of Jerusalem with the land of Samaria lying between them.

The United Monarchy of Israel was the kingdom of Israel established in 1050 BCE under the reign of Saul. It continued under kings David and Solomon. Shortly after the death of Solomon in 930 BCE, Israel, under the incompetent kingship of Solomon's son Rehoboam divided into the northern kingdom of Israel and the southern kingdom of Judah. Galilee was part of the northern kingdom.

During the next two hundred years there were skirmishes between the divided kingdoms and much of the surviving history as contained in the Hebrew Scriptures was written by people of Judah. In 732, Tiglath-Pileser III, king of Assyria, conquered and destroyed Israel and parts of Judah, but did not take Jerusalem. Samaria and Galilee were completely depopulated, peasantry and elites alike. The Assyrians resettled Samaria with non-Jews from other areas of their empire. As recorded in 2 Kgs 17:24, "The king of Assyria brought people from Babylon, Cuthah, Avva, Hamath, and Sepharvaim, and placed them in the cities of Samaria in place of the people of Israel; they took possession of Samaria, and settled in its cities." Their intent was to create a buffer between their empire and rival Egypt. Further, 2 Kgs makes no mention of Galilee being resettled in this way. The archaeological evidence indicates that after its destruction Galilee was not repopulated. It literally remained vacant for the next two hundred years.[1] In the sixth century BCE a few small isolated communities formed, but there was no significant settlement until the first century BCE.

In Judah the story is different. In the sixth century BCE the Babylonians laid siege to Jerusalem and subsequently destroyed the Temple and burned Jerusalem. The city's elites were taken into captivity in what is now referred to as "The Exile." The Persians under Cyrus defeated the Babylonians and in 538 BCE the exiled Judeans were permitted to return to Judah and re-build their Temple, but still paid tribute to Persia. In 331 BCE the Persians were conquered by Alexander the Great and Judah came under control of the Greeks and their successive Seleucid dynasty. Israel remained a vassal state under foreign domination for just short of four hundred years. During those centuries some Jews remained loyal to the temple cult. Others became acculturated to the foreign influences. When the Seleucid king Antiochus IV Epiphanes forced Hellenization on the Jews, including forbidding Jewish cult practices, e.g., honoring the Sabbath and circumcision, the Jews revolted. In 164 BCE the Judean Maccabees captured Jerusalem and established the mostly independent Hasmonean Dynasty in Judah. While still paying some tribute to the Seleucids, Judah largely came under its own rule.

During this period, out of a group of scribes and sages emerged a new group that became known as the Pharisees or "separate ones." They were separate in terms of their strong belief in following the "purity laws," which had been part of Temple service. They also adhered to a set of detailed extensions to the Torah known as the verbal law or tradition of the elders. In the beginning, the Pharisees were supporters of the Hasmonean dynasty, but under the Priest-King John Hyrcanus a split occurred. Hyrcanus dis-solved the purity laws of the Pharisees and punished those who practiced them. Under John's two sons, expansion continued. Aristobulus ruled for one year and died, and his brother, Alexander Jannaeus, became Priest-King and ruled from 103 to 76 BCE. There was a great deal of internal conflict during Jannaeus's rule. His military exploits placed considerable burden on the Judean citizenry, causing him to face substantial resistance from the populace. He took up with where his father left off with the Phari-sees. Around the year 88 BCE Jannaeus reportedly had eight hundred of

---

1. Gal, *Lower Galilee*, 108.

the dissident Pharisees crucified, but not before he had the throats of the Pharisees' wives and children slashed in their presence. By now Samaria and Galilee were completely in Israel's orbit and in the first century BCE Galilee began to be repopulated. Recent archaeological discoveries of synagogues have shown the development of the Jewish identity during this and later periods in Galilee, a topic to which we will now turn.

Solidifying the Jewish Identity

Around the time of Jannaeus, perhaps a bit earlier, another significant undertaking began. Up until the Hasmonean rebellion the Jews in Judea varied in their commitment to the Temple cult and Jewish practice. Evidence from archaeology indicates that fine tableware, select wines, and other luxury goods were imported into the area. For the most part this now came to a halt. The Judean population, whether under the influence of the Pharisees or others, began to adhere to purity laws which had been used as preparation for temple rituals rather than personal commitments. Trade outside of Judea practically ceased. New fine imported tableware and wines from surrounding areas are rarely found in first century BCE and first century CE sites. The period was also characterized by a lack of artwork depicting living creatures. But distinctive clay vessels of simplistic design manufactured from local clays came into common use. Step-down immersion pools (miqwaoth) began to appear in private homes of the wealthy and communal pools served the general population in the cities and villages. Stone cups and bowls, believed less likely to become impure, have been found in the ruins of households throughout Galilee. Knife cut simple design clay lamps manufactured in or near Jerusalem become the standard in Jewish homes. After being ruled by foreign powers for centuries and now free to form their own unique identity, the people of Judea and Galilee began to solidify their identity as a religion and as a nation. In this process, the Pharisees taught that salvation required more than commitment to the Temple cult. It now required personal dedication to ritual purity in the home and daily life.[2]

2. Berlin, "Manifest Identity," 151; Mattila, "Inner Life," 312.

Who Actually Migrated to Repopulate Galilee?

Archaeological evidence makes two things clear. First, the sudden creation of new towns and villages in Galilee during this period is indicative of substantial in-migration. There is no reasonable explanation that could justify growth of this magnitude by internal population growth. Second, the remains of archaeological sites undeniably indicate these people were Jews. Archaeological evidence for the period indicated that the migrants were Jews from Judah. The proof comes in the form of period coins of Judah, stone vessels, stepped immersion pools, burial practices following Judean practice, and Judean lamps all found at Galilean archaeological sites.[3] The presence of stone vessels and stepped immersion pools for practicing purity rituals were nearly identical in both Judea and Galilee. Remnants of knife cut lamps from Jerusalem are pervasive in Galilean ruins from this period. The serious migration to Galilee started under Jannaeus's reign late in the second century BCE and continued well into the first century CE. Hasmonean veteran soldiers and increasing demographic pressure of young landless males working on royal estates were ripe for emigration to the fertile valleys and fresh water lakes of Galilee. Additionally, the creation of new farm land in the north created additional tax revenues to support Jannaeus's lavish lifestyle and military ventures which included unending civil disobedience and war with neighboring states. Many in Judea at this time fled to Damascus and Egypt. Others, displeased with the religious tone set in Judea and the political opponents of Jannaeus, but not wishing to leave their Jewish culture, found migration to Galilee an attractive alternative. It is not a stretch to think that some of these may well have been Pharisees. The migration from Judah lasted well into the first century CE after the Romans captured the region.

Then Came the Romans and Herodians

The Hasmonean Dynasty ended in 63 BCE with the Roman military under Pompey conquering the region. A few decades later Rome appointed Herod as King of the Jews and bestowed upon him Roman citizenship. It has been argued that this excused him and his descendants from paying the Roman tribute.[4] Roman policy frequently offered ruling elites favors

3. Reed, *Archaeology and the Galilean Jesus*, 44.
4. Udoh, "Taxation," 366–87.

and favorable tax conditions to maintain their loyalty with expectations for certain favors in return. Herod earned the title "Great" for his many building projects such as the port of Caesarea and the rebuilding and expansion of the Temple. Many objected to the heavy taxation required to support these building projects. Further dissatisfaction centered on his building of the Roman styled city of Caesarea in honor of the Roman Emperor (one of those honorific favors mentioned above). As was typical for despots, Herod dealt with his detractors ruthlessly, including three of his sons whom he had executed. At his death, the area under Herod's rule was divided between three of his remaining sons. Philip received the far northeastern sectors, Antipas received Galilee and Perea, and Archelaus received Judah, Samaria, and Idumea. Soon after Herod's death, an appeal was made to Archelaus in Jerusalem for redress from taxation and imprisonment of dissenters who had protested the execution of martyrs who had taken down an eagle statue from the Temple mount. While the meeting began well, it turned ugly and resulted in violence and a mass killing of the petitioners. This led to insurrection throughout Judea and Galilee.

Around the year 34 BCE Hezekiah, a bandit and rebel, overran the Galilean countryside. After some initial successes Hezekiah was captured and subsequently executed by Herod. Thirty years later his son Judas stormed and captured the military garrison at Sepphoris, at the time Galilee's major military installation. The Romans took a dim view of Judas's rebellious attitude. Roman legions swept down through the Galilean countryside, destroying villages, laying waste to Sepphoris, and killing or selling many of its residents into slavery. Herod's son Archelaus was removed from his duties in 6 CE and the provinces of Judea, Samaria, and Idumea came under the direct control of a Roman prelate or governor. Galilee, however, remained under Herod's son often referred to as Herod Antipas, but hereafter referred to as simply Antipas.

Since Sepphoris was just a short distance from Nazareth it is unlikely that the villagers of Nazareth escaped this assault unscathed. Josephus, the Jewish historian, wrote that the rebellion ended with two thousand of the rebels crucified along the roadsides for miles. Josephus is known for exaggerating numbers and overstating Rome's power, but regardless, the rebellion did not end well for the rebels. It is also clear that Rome's strategy for controlling client states was to co-opt the local aristocracy, engage them in administering local rule, and threaten brutal retaliation for any slight infraction in order to discourage resistance and nascent rebellion. Sepphoris is an example that made the threat material. Crucifixion was their ultimate tool of brutality. It not only led to an excruciating death, but also public humiliation while one was still alive on the cross and the indignity of having one's lifeless body torn apart by birds of prey and roaming animals after death.

The destruction of Galilee in 4 BCE left many homeless and destitute. Families were fractured as the men were killed and the women raped and/ or sold into slavery. Some escaped into the surrounding hills and survived by turning to banditry. They hid in area caves or melted incognito into local villages after swarming out of the countryside to attack Roman supply lines or an aristocrat's manor. These early guerilla tactics often had the sympathy and support of local citizens and was a harassing form of insurgency directed at the Romans and Jewish aristocracy.[5]

It is unclear as to the whereabouts of Joseph, Mary, and Jesus at the time of this destruction. If we were to take the Gospels as historically accurate, the Gospel of Luke would have them back in Nazareth since he has them returning to Nazareth a short time after the birth narrative. The Gospel of Matthew, on the other hand, has them living in Bethlehem at the time of the birth, Herod getting word of the birth, and then ordering all children two years and younger to be murdered. Joseph, Mary, and Jesus go into exile in Egypt to escape this threat. When Herod dies they get word and return. But to avoid living under the rule of the less-than-amiable Archelaus, they divert their travels and settle in Nazareth under the rule of Antipas. Matthew's account clearly draws a parallel between the birth of Jesus and the birth of Moses as it is recounted in Hebrew tradition, and therefore may be more allegoric than historic. Both accounts satisfy the need for Jesus to be born in Bethlehem of Judea providing an undergirding for messianic claims made later in the Gospels. That being said, Joseph, Mary, and Jesus would have either experienced the horrors of Sepphoris or known friends or relatives who had.

Galilean Power Politics

In the time of Jesus, Rome was the supreme power. It had conquered most of the known world and had brought the Pax Romana, the Roman Peace, to the region. But as Crossan has pointed out it is a peace dictated on the basis of violence. It is an absence of wide-scale rebellion enforced through superior military might. We saw this a few pages back when rebellion in Galilee

5. Horsley, *Bandits, Prophets, and Messiahs*, 67–69.

led to the destruction of Sepphoris. There appears to be little evidence of permanent Roman presence in Galilee in the first half of the first century CE—either military or civilian.[6] However, military forces were available in nearby Syria should the occasion call for them.

Rome maintained control over its provinces and client states in two primary ways. First, whenever possible they identified an aristocratic class they could empower to rule the province for them. Such was the case with Herod. It was also the continuing case for some time for his sons Antipas, Philip, and Archelaus. But after the insurrection mentioned earlier, Archelaus was deposed and Rome went to plan B and installed a governor to oversee Judea and its companion areas. At the time of Jesus's crucifixion, the Roman governor was Pontius Pilot.

The center of Jewish religion, of course, was Jerusalem of Judea. It was the gathering point for Jews throughout the empire to celebrate various Jewish religious days, the most noteworthy being Passover. It should not go unnoticed that Passover was a celebration of Jewish independence from the pharaohs of Egypt. During this time Jerusalem's population swelled to many times its natural state. It was during Passover that disruptions had occurred in the past. Thus there was a strong Roman military presence at hand to deal with any such disturbances that might occur during these Jewish holy days.

Rome established and maintained the allegiance of places like Galilee under a client ruler by cutting a good deal for the ruling elite. Further, Rome did not have a one-or-two-sizes-fit-all solution to maintaining allegiance. Rather, Rome cut deals that seemed likely to work for each individual situation.[7] As for Galilee under Antipas, while the threat of Roman power was always a consideration, as long as Antipas remained loyal and kept restless natives pacified, the Romans kept their distance. One of the ways they maintained allegiance was by keeping tax burdens they placed on client rulers low enough to leave room for the client ruler to pursue his own agenda.[8] As we saw earlier, Antipas as the son of Herod was a citizen. He was educated in Rome and knew the Roman elites quite well. In addition, as Herod's heir, Galilee under Antipas's rule may have been exempt from the Roman tribute as we indicated a bit earlier. The same would have been true for Judea initially, but once Archelaus was deposed and a Roman governor installed the tribute would have again been operative.

6. Reed, *Archaeology and the Galilean Jesus*, 217.

7. Berlin, "Manifest Identity," 171.

8. Mattingly, "Imperial Economy," 287.

Antipas was politically forced to walk that thin line between keeping the peace in a predominantly Jewish state and at the same time satisfying the expectations of the Roman hegemony. How did he do this? For one thing, Rome expected to be honored in the local provinces through various memorials. Antipas did this by rebuilding Sepphoris in the design of a Greco-Roman city and then even more so in building Tiberias and naming it after the emperor. But at the same time this was done he was very careful not to offend Jewish sensibilities. All the households and symbols of the new Judaism were present. Additionally, no art depicting human bodies or bodies of other living creatures have been found in archaeological sites. Galilee was a Jewish enclave in the Roman world, perhaps even more so than Judea with its more obvious Roman presence.

Finally, it should not go unmentioned that Galilee had its own independent spirit. Recall it was settled by people leaving the crowded areas of Judea. Many immigrated to escape its uncivil political climate of the time. This is borne out by the insurrection of 4 BCE in Galilee, the presence of bandits and brigands before and after that time, and the ferment that was in Galilee prior to the First Roman War (66–73 CE) that led to the destruction of the Temple. This has led some to believe that a certain amount of tension existed between Galileans and Judeans. The latter felt superior and perhaps even jealous of the more independent and prosperous Galileans. Judeans were perhaps a bit more polished, spoke the "correct" dialogue, and were more pious in their religious practice.

Within this context we must not forget how brutal this society could be. Remember, Antipas, probably in a drunken stupor, had John the Baptist's head brought on a platter into a celebration to please his stepdaughter. Nor should we forget the crucifixions practiced not only by the Romans, but also by the Hasmonean Alexander Jannaeus. The history of exploitation was endemic in ancient kingdoms. One only need recount the cries of the prophets for justice in the land. Or need only read Neh 5 to see the pain that Israelite elites inflicted on the less powerful after their return from exile in the sixth century CE. It is an ancient story. The powerful exploit the weaker and the weaker hasten to do the bidding of the powerful, until it gets so unbearable that the weaker rebel.

Galilean Family Politics

The topic of politics would be incomplete if we did not have at least a brief discussion of family politics. In first-century Galilee the family unit was of supreme importance. This is especially true among the commoners whose family unit struggled to be above subsistence living, especially in difficult years. In Appendix II we will explore the economy of Galilee in more depth, but at this point it is important to note that the family unit was the primary "bread winners" making life possible. Often the family units would combine into extended family units with connected housing and shared courtyards that served as extensions to their small living units. Intermarriage of cousins was frequent as a way of keeping the family's resources contained within a common family unit. As with all family and extended family units one's personal allegiance was first and foremost to the familial unit and then perhaps to other village dwellers. Within each family unit the eldest male served the role of the family patriarch who set the tone and passed on both family and religious traditions. Any malady that fell upon a productive family member could bring dysfunction if not disaster to the family unit itself. There also appear to be social stratification between family units. This is evident from archaeological findings of different housing forms which we will delve into in Appendix II. From several biblical references critiquing Jesus for whom he ate with and associated and the pressure to adhere to the Pharisaic purity laws leads to a conclusion that social strata and outward appearances played an important role in how one and one's clan were viewed and placed in the first-century social hierarchy. It is this inwardly focused family unity and social stratification that Jesus worked to change by sharing love for all of God's humanity.

In Appendix II we will continue our analysis of life in first-century CE Galilee, but proceed with a portrait of the Galilean economy, its public health conditions, and its prevailing religious beliefs. This will set up the background in which the ministry of Jesus played out.

Appendix II

Economy, Public Health, and Religion Matrix of First-Century Galilee

WHILE HISTORICAL BACKDROP AND political arrangements provide some insight into Galilean life during our period of interest, they do not tell the whole story. The state of the economic and general health conditions also play important roles, as do prevailing religious belief. In many descriptions of this time period these factors have either been overly simplified or completely ignored. Nevertheless, they make up important components of the first-century context.

The Economy of First-Century Galilee

Until recently the Galilean economy has been described as dirt poor farmers being exploited by wealthy city-dweller elites. It has been believed to be an economy that worked for 10 percent of the population who were able to gain access to farmers' surpluses through heavy taxation consisting of the Roman tribute, taxes to pay for Antipas's aggressive building programs and the Temple tax. As the farmers got deeper in debt they ultimately sold their property to pay their taxes and farmed their former land as tenants or moved to the cities and became day laborers. While this probably did occur to a significant extent, it is not the complete picture. For one thing, much of the understanding of first-century Galilee has come from biblical studies supplemented with the writings of Flavius Josephus, the first-century Jewish historian, and from sociological models. One drawback to this is that the biblical accounts have been largely Judah-centric. However, Judah and Galilee had very different historical backgrounds. Galilee had a much younger economy. While the economy was perhaps still subject to ancient hierarchical and elitism forces, it was also more dynamic, where demand and supply played a greater role in determining outcomes than in its southern neighbor. Also, Judah came under direct Roman control in 6 CE while Galilee didn't until 44 CE. Some have argued that resulted in less of a tax burden in Galilee that may have lessened the indebtedness of farmers in Judah.[1] In fact, Antipas, as the son of Herod the Great who was granted Roman citizenship, may have been excused from the Roman tribute,[2] which would have lessened strains in Galilee and left more resources for the development of such projects as rebuilding Sepphoris and the construction of Tiberias. Thus, it is important to not uncritically project conditions prevalent in first-century Judah onto the Galilean context.

Archaeological reports in the last few decades indicate that the cities of Sepphoris and Tiberias contained many wealthy households. But the towns and villages outside these cities also had pockets of wealth and archaeological excavations in these areas provide evidence to support the existence of families across a socioeconomic spectrum. "The archaeological excavations at both first century northern towns of Yodefat and Gamla show that most of their inhabitants lived their lives between levels of prosperity and simplicity, but not poverty. The different types of finds do not suggest the existence of an impoverished population, but rather a population of medium and high social ranks."[3] Additionally, analyses of skeletal remains found of the local peoples massacred in the Roman affront on Galilee leading up to the destruction of the Temple in Jerusalem in 70 CE indicate a populous that was in relatively good health having few signs of malnutrition, poor sanitation, or severe disease before they died.[4]

Galilee had rich agricultural areas. In these areas many villagers could subsist on agricultural production. In these communities housing tended to be tightly constructed with abutting walls around meandering unplanned streets. These villages were typically not walled and their agricultural fields and terraces were located outside the villages with plots marked off by stones or short walls. During the repopulation it is believed that Galilee was made up of many small plot farms that practiced diversity in small scale agriculture. Galilee has within its territory five different soil types that

1. Fiensy, "Assessing the Economy," 169.
2. Udoh, "Taxation," 371.
3. Aviam, "Socio-economical Hierarchy," 30.
4. Ibid., 36.

are suitable for different crops.[5] The farm families often owned land that was not contiguous and was located in different types of soil. To an extent feasible, farmers grew the crops that were most suitable for the soil available to them. This gave them diversity in crop yields spreading their risk of crop failure over several crops and spreading harvest workloads over the different crop cycles. Farmers also had the ability to let some fields lie fallow in certain periods to rejuvenate the soil. Roads during this time were primitive and little more than foot paths connecting the towns and villages. Transportation was by donkey or camel, slow and methodical, and very expensive. As a result of this, products did not travel far distances to be sold or bartered. Cities such as Sepphoris and Tiberius were strategically built close to agricultural lands and water resources that could supply them.

But some areas in northern Galilee were rocky and mountainous and not at all suitable for raising crops. These towns and villages survived and prospered on a mix of herding and manufacturing along with some crop raising. In time these tended to be more prosperous than the crop-raising-only communities. While the manufacture of olive oil was a lucrative business, it was not as ubiquitous in Galilee as many earlier have thought.[6] Manufacturing tended to focus on items needed for daily use such as woolens manufactured in Khirbet Qana (i.e., ancient Cana) and clay pottery and stone vessels manufactured in Kefar Hananya and Shikhin. According to the archaeologist Mordechai Avian, "It seems that in a creative way, Jews in mountainous Galilee adapted themselves to the geographical conditions of rocky terrain and lack of arable land. As their agricultural land was poor, they developed wool and textile industry along with pottery production."[7]

The variability in first-century houses excavated in Galilee is indicative of a diversity of wealth or socioeconomic status in these towns and villages. The simplest form of housing was the terrace home of one or perhaps two rooms, with homes having abutting walls and a shared courtyard. These housing complexes would typically be shared by an extended family. A step up was independent housing with a dedicated side courtyard. The most luxurious would be an independent home with an internal courtyard. In the major cities homes for the wealthiest may have internal courtyards and several rooms, and perhaps multiple stories. But even the wealthiest Galileans did not demonstrate the opulence found in the coastal cities or

5. Choi, "Never the Two Shall Meet?," 301.

6. Aviam, "Socio-economical Hierarchy," 33.

7. Ibid., 35.

the mansions of Jerusalem.[8] However, the presence of these manufacturing towns and villages near the outskirts of Sepphoris and Tiberius speaks to an active trade economy in which the manufacturers sold and traded their goods. Thus, the economy of first-century Galilee was much more complex and consisted of socioeconomic strata beyond the simplistic peasant/elite dualism previously depicted.

Aviam proposes three social strata that existed in first-century Galilee.[9] The lowest strata were the dayworkers, shepherds, and beggars. Perhaps Harvard Professor Elisabeth Schüssler Fiorenza would add the so-called sinners to these lowest strata. This includes lower-level tax collectors, prostitutes, pimps, fruit sellers, swineherders, garlic peddlers, bartenders, seamen, public announcers, servants, the crippled, and criminals. In short, all those so poorly paid, marginal, desperate, and abused—the scum of Palestinian society.[10] That is, the one's Jesus associated with and *invited to the table*. Perhaps slightly above them or at the same station were the potters, spinners, weavers, and simple farmers either working for others or owning their own small plot. The second level consisted of business owners of the small workshops producing olive oil, flour, and woven goods, and the more skilled workers including blacksmiths, carpenters, and skilled stone workers. At the top of the social strata would be merchants, agricultural middlemen, families of the oligarchy, tax collector overseers, and other officials in Antipas's government, including the military.

The building of the cities of Sepphoris and Tiberius no doubt had an impact on the population composition of Galilee. Prior to Herod's death he ruled all the areas that his sons Antipas, Philip, and Archelaus subsequently inherited. After his father's death Antipas put in his own administration for Galilee and Perea, which undoubtedly placed greater administrative costs on these populations. Further, the building of the cities brought to Galilee builders, planners, administrators, soldiers, all of which substantially decreased the ratio of agricultural to nonagricultural workers. This placed greater productivity demands on the farmer and the land. Additionally, the Romans brought advances in agriculture to their subject provinces. These included crop specialization, irrigation, and some degree of land consolidation. Crop specialization that works for larger estates is riskier for small plot farmers. A

---

8. Fiensy, "Galilean Village," 201.

9. Aviam, "Socio-economical Hierarchy," 37.

10. Schüssler Fiorenza, *In Memory of Her*, 128.

bad crop, draught, insect infestation, all of which were frequent, could result in starvation, increasing debt, and perhaps ultimately loss of property.

Further, the construction programs of Antipas placed an additional tax burden beyond that required for funding his administrative and military bureaucracies. For example, it has been estimated that Sepphoris and Tiberius had planned streets in a grid pattern with a main street over 40 feet wide, formally designed market places, large public buildings, and large domestic quarters. Tiberius had an athletic stadium, monumental gate, perhaps a gymnasium, and a hippodrome for horse and chariot racing. Sepphoris had a large basilica that functioned as a governmental building for its administration and courts. The cities also had aqueducts constructed to supply them with adequate water.[11] Through all of this, one thing is clear: the picture is much more complex than a Galilee of a very few city elites taking advantage of peasant farmers and driving them into dispossession of land and livelihood.

Antipas, like his predecessors, minted low-value coins. These were undoubtedly used for low-volume trade. Both Sepphoris and Tiberias had large areas set aside for markets. Each of the cities had administrative officials (agoranomoi) responsible for determining the accuracy of weights and measures. They also had responsibility for setting prices. This has led some speculation that the markets were inherently unfair to producers and leaned to advantage the city buyers. However, with other options of manufacturing and herding available to citizens, price exploitation by these officials would have been limited.

Before leaving this topic mention should be made of the general level of education in this economy. Truthfully, very little is known. There appears to be little archaeological evidence for schooling during the first century CE. It has been argued that schooling was done in the synagogues or within the home. We do know that the state of the economy did require legal documents to be drawn up for the loaning of money, transfer of land, and other common business transactions. Clearly these functions required literacy in the populace no matter how limited. This created a need for a social class known as the scribes who worked not only in the Temple in Jerusalem but functioned throughout Palestine, including Galilee. Biblical scholar John Poirier has argued that the limited presence of inscriptions found in Galilee may not be indicative of widespread illiteracy, but rather that common education focused on reading skills (i.e., for reading the Torah), but did not

11. Fiensy, "Galilean Village," 192.

include writing skills.[12] Writing may have been part of the education of the priests and scribes, but not the general population. That would certainly square with the Gospel's accounts of Jesus's familiarity with the Scriptures and the recollection of him reading from Isaiah recorded in Luke 4:16–22.

While Galilee showed signs of growth and development, the building of Sepphoris, Tiberius, and general urbanization of the region brought new challenges to the economy of Galilee, creating both opportunity and risk. There were winners and there were losers in Antipas's economy. Some of the winners were in the cities, some in villages, especially in those villages with a mix of manufacturing and agricultural activity. Further, his building projects provided employment, stimulated trade, and in general raised the level of prosperity.[13] Some losers were in the country. Many lost their land due to debt burden and foreclosure, and were forced to work as tenant farmers or migrate to the cities to become day workers or even beggars. It was a time of change and mobility within Galilee itself. Literacy was limited to the scribal and priestly actors, but some ability to read may have been present in the broader population. Next we will consider the impact of health issues on inhabitants of first century Galilee.

Public Health in Galilee

Why public health in Galilee? That may seem to be an unusual departure from politics and economy. Yet it is very closely related, especially to the economy. The general health of the populace in first-century Galilee, or for anywhere else for that matter, was poor. Not only was it poor but it was critical to the viability of the smallest economic unit: the family. As healthy as the economy may have been in Galilee, it was all relative. The great majority of Galileans still lived at just above or below subsistence level, depending on the agricultural crop year or trading year for manufactured goods. The death or sickness of any key family member, particularly the patriarch, meant the difference between life as usual and destitution.

Perhaps reviewing some of the living conditions of the time will provide insight. Soap had not yet been invented; in cities, sewers for the most part were open trenches into which chamber pots were dumped drawing mosquitoes, flies, and other vermin; life expectancy at birth was less than thirty years; and women were often afflicted by infections resulting from

12. Poirier, "Education/Literacy in Jewish Galilee," 255–56.

13. Aviam, "People, Land, Economy, and Belief," 20.

frequent childbirth events.[14] Country folk did not fare much better. Living in close proximity to their animal stock, working fields in lower lands with malaria invested mosquitoes, and engaging in manual labor in which the slightest scratch could lead to deadly infection left this group equally susceptible to poor health and early death. All of this plus the economic insecurities it and other forces exerted resulted in a very high migration and internal mobility rate within Galilee.

Jonathan Reed agrees with the high mobility rates within Galilee. "Chronic and seasonal disease, especially malaria, cut down significant segments of the populations and left even the seemingly healthy quite often ill. Galilee in the wake of the Hasmonean conquest and Antipas's urbanization projects witnessed considerable internal migration."[15] Urbanization and placing heavier demands on the agricultural sector to feed the cities, forced less productive lower lands into use which were the breeding grounds for malaria carrying mosquito. Death and disability wreaked havoc on the economic viability of families during this period. "Life expectancy according to age at death tomb inscriptions in Rome indicates a median age of death at 23 years. In upper Galilee examined bones from the era indicate that 50 percent of the deaths occurred prior to reaching adulthood and 70 percent of those within the first few years of life."[16] Much of this became a vicious cycle. Poor health created instability. Malaria cut down personal productivity and increased the occurrences of anemia. Lower harvests led to less food, poorer nutrition, and higher susceptibility to further disease. "Sudden death, rampant disease, frequent pregnancy, and increasing migration made for an unstable environment with volatile households whose compositions were constantly and abruptly changing."[17]

Before leaving this topic we would be remiss not to discuss one more malady of the first century. Leviticus 13:45–46 contains the following statement regarding leprosy: "The person who has the leprous disease shall wear torn clothes and let the hair of his head be disheveled; and he shall cover his upper lip and cry out, 'Unclean, unclean.' He shall remain unclean as long as he has the disease; he is unclean. He shall live alone; his dwelling shall be outside the camp." Each of the three Synoptic Gospels recounts Jesus healing a leper. Before we get too far into this discussion we should make

14. Stark, *Rise of Christianity*, 152–54.
15. Reed, "Mortality," 242.
16. Ibid., 243.
17. Ibid., 250.

it clear that this disease, translated as leprosy, was not what we know as leprosy today. In fact, for the period, "Archaeologists have found no human remains in Palestine showing signs of leprosy."[18] What has been translated as leprosy was practically any skin condition brought on probably by a dry climate and lack of sanitation. Today we might call it psoriasis or eczema. While our victim suffering from "leprosy" was not likely to have his or her nose, fingers, or toes dropping off soon, the consequences were even greater. It caused great embarrassment for one's family and deprived it of a productive worker. For the afflicted it meant deep humiliation and the end of life as it had been, at least temporarily, if not permanently. John Dominic Crossan distinguishes between a disease and an illness. A disease in his view is something physical that has a deteriorating effect on the body. That would be psoriasis or eczema. The illness is the psychological impact it has on the individual and the sociological response of the community.[19] The latter would consist of the personal shame of being declared unclean, the humiliation of appearing disheveled and shouting "unclean, unclean," and the social disgrace expressed by ones family and peers.

Religion in Galilee

A few things at this point seem clear. First of all, while this section focuses on religion, in the first century it was impossible to separate religion from all other aspects of life. Secondly, while there were common Jewish practices, there was no unified Jewish religion. The Sadducees who populated much of the priestly and administrative positions operated the Temple rituals. The Essenes took purity laws to extremes, divorced themselves from the Temple, and practiced Judaism in "its truest form" away from the corrupt Temple culture. The Pharisees took a more centrist position. They were not as extreme as the Essenes, but indeed did proclaim the purity laws as understood from the tradition of the elders, also known as the oral tradition. The scribes were the literate ones that worked in the Temple or within the community. They were teachers and interpreters of the law out of which the Pharisees originated.

While there may have been many Jewish approaches the more salient question is if there was a normative Jewish viewpoint. That is, was there a viewpoint that the vast majority of the people admired and personally

18. Korb, *Life in Year One*, 114.

19. Crossan, *Jesus*, 81–82.

followed, at least to some extent? Further, if there was, who were the initiators and teachers of this "common Judaism"? Roland Deines has made a persuasive argument that there was a common Judaism of the time and that it was promulgated by the Pharisees who were widely respected among the populous.[20] This is consistent with the Gospel's eighty-nine references to this group. It is also consistent with the widening gap between the "people" and the temple cult in Jerusalem, which lost the trust of people as far back as the Hasmoneans, combining the political leadership with the religious leadership that led to the separate movements of the Essenes and Pharisees.

What is it that the Pharisees taught? First and foremost it was the tradition of the elders. This was an extensive effort to identify how one was to live in concert with the Torah. The justification was said to come from oral instruction given by Moses at Mount Horeb. In reality it probably developed in or shortly after the return from the Exile. It roots are in a theology which basically holds that one gets what they deserve. It is what Walter Brueggemann has called the great "if clause" of Deut 28.[21] You are blessed among nations if you follow God's commandments. On the other hand, if you don't, look out! It will not be pleasant. As Duet 28:20 puts is, "The Lord will send upon you disaster, panic, and frustration in everything you attempt to do, until you are destroyed and perish quickly, on account of the evil of your deeds, because you have forsaken me."

And that is just about what happened. In 587, Jerusalem had been destroyed, its elite taken into captivity, and its Temple demolished. The tradition of the elders became the oral guidelines of how to live day to day within the broader and more abstract outline of the Torah. The underlying logic was to preclude such punishment from coming again. It was to be Israel's salvation. The logic of the "tradition" can be illustrated as follows: the Torah says—"the seventh day is a Sabbath to the Lord your God; you shall not do any work" (Exod 20:10). The tradition of the elders would expand upon this, and say, for example: "The work of the physician is to heal; therefore healing on the Sabbath is forbidden."

A second element of the Pharisaic initiative was to extend the purity laws of the Temple to all Jews. This is what we saw earlier with step down emersion pools in homes and communities, and the proliferation of stone vessels for food preparation. Teaching and proclaiming the tradition of the

20. Deines, "Pharisees," 503–4.
21. Brueggemann, *Chosen?*, 29.

elders was the Pharisees' attempt to bring piety, and in their view salvation, to the entire Jewish people and thus find God's favor.

It is illustrative to note how many of the proverbs of the wisdom literature reinforce this theology. For example, consider Prov 10:4, "A slack hand causes poverty, but the hand of the diligent makes rich." Or Prov 10:26, "Like vinegar to the teeth, and smoke to the eyes, so are the lazy to their employers." Or Prov 113:10, "Misfortune pursues sinners, but prosperity rewards the righteous." These three, and there are many more, all have the common theme that whatever outcome one experiences, good or bad, it was deserved, and the direct result of their righteous or sinful behavior. There was no thought of systemic exploitation, only personal success or failure. One need please God, or suffer the consequences.

About the time of the forming of the Pharisees, during the Hasmonean dynasty, another view arose, the apocalyptic. It was an outcome of the treachery of Antiochus Epiphanes who made every effort to Hellenize the Jews including slaughtering a pig on the Temple alter and forbidding circumcision at the point of the sword. Here it was not Israel's sinful actions being punished, but rather the righteous being slaughtered for their faithful practice. Chapters 7–12 of the Book of Daniel vividly describes a vision and then explains it, illustrating the terror Israel had suffered under various regimes since the Exile up to the actions of Antiochus Epiphanes. His vision saw the principalities of this world being destroyed and replaced with an eternal rule. In his vision, God wipes the old dominions of exploitation away and a new everlasting kingdom is established on earth under the reign of a son of man. All is finally made right for those who have suffered righteously and in God's behalf. It is not clear who wrote the apocalypse. It may have been the Essenes, but it was not the prevailing message of the Pharisees.

Religion, Politics, Economy, and Public Health

The scenario is now set for Jesus coming on the scene. Politically, many, but not all, Galileans chafed under the yoke of Antipas and his Roman overseers. If trouble was to occur anywhere in Palestine, a safe bet would be that it had its origins in Galilee. That no doubt stemmed from the types of people who resettled the area: young landless males, retired soldiers who had earlier captured the land, Pharisees, Pharisee sympathizers, and others fleeing the wrath of the latter Hasmonean leadership. Galileans, while obliged to honor and celebrate the various religious holidays held in Jerusalem, were also somewhat estranged from the Temple cult and Jerusalem's culture. They viewed themselves as pious Jews honoring the purity laws, although not with the fervor of the Pharisees and certainly not the Essenes. But it was enough for them to adopt the immersion pools, stone vessels, and related aids for maintaining purity. They also apparently relished the outward expression of their Jewish identity by keeping to the simply designed yet functional pottery, lamps void of decoration, and any symbolic or artistic likenesses of living creatures.

Economically, their religion held the predominate view that their place in society was what they deserved. The wealthy could easily justify their wealth with the wisdom literature of Proverbs and prevailing theology as well as look down on the less fortunate as being deserving of their lot in life. That is not to say that there were not countervailing calls from the earlier prophets calling for compassion and justice for the dispossessed, the alien, widow, and orphan. Also a growing body, the apocalyptic literature, which was perhaps inspired by the second half of Daniel, and some wisdom literature such as Ecclesiastes and Job, began to challenge the view that misfortune was the act of God showing displeasure for the victim's sinfulness.

Similar views could be promulgated for the many health issues of the day. Death and ill health were endemic in the population. In an economy where many lived just above subsistence in the best years, loss of a productive member could mean the difference between surviving or not for the nuclear family. Some maladies were thought to be particularly disdainful in God's eyes. Leprosy as it was defined in those days was one of them. In the theology of the time, lepers obviously deserved their affliction and no one had the right to provide them with assistance and thus work counter to God's will.

It is into what most of us would describe as the very bleak circumstance of the day that Jesus was born, grew to maturity, ministered, and taught. It is the brutal society in which even the slightest critique of power and following by commoners could get one lifted up and hung on a cross.

Study Guide

The Adult Discussion Class

THIS SECTION SHARES GUIDELINES for leading an adult discussion group drawn from both behavioral science and my own experience in leading similar groups. Some of it will be "old hat" for seasoned group leaders, but to others it may offer a blueprint for leading a successful adult seminar. Best wishes with forming your group.

Physical Setting

Arrange the seating so everyone can see other group members. If possible a large table or tables arranged in a square or rectangle will suffice. If tables are not an option seating in a circle will also work well. Whenever possible avoid individuals seated behind one another. Also, whenever possible, arrange for a meeting space that does not have traffic passing through or around it and where there are minimal distractions. This book does not require use of audiovisual equipment. However, other study materials may require a large screen television with DVD and/or computer inputs. Computer projection equipment is also a nice addition for some class material. Note: when using audiovisual equipment always check it out ahead of time with a practice run before the class. This may be obvious, but my experience has been that when technology is being used there is more often than not a glitch. Glitches can routinely be avoided with test setups and practice runs.

Administrative Structure

For the class to run seamlessly there needs to be a class organizer who will take primary leadership responsibility. Those responsibilities include the following:

1. Form a Planning Group: The planning group selects study materials. This class organizer should invite all class members to join the planning group. Typically, only a few will volunteer and generally a group size of five to seven is more efficient. But it is important for each class member to feel that they are welcome to take part in the planning if they should desire to do so. Set a time for the planning group to meet that works for everyone. Each member is encouraged to recommend study materials and if possible bring them to the meeting. Individuals participating should recommend only material they have personally reviewed. Only in rare situations have I found it to be productive for someone to suggest material they have not read and therefore cannot effectively vouch for. The class organizer should always have at least two to three books or material resources to recommend. It is often helpful to use online book store reviews and author biographies as supplementary information to help make study material decisions. The planning group should meet with ample time prior to the first class session to ensure that study materials will be available prior to the first class.

2. Select Materials: Select books or other material that can be readily divided into weekly sessions. For a book, normally chapters of ten to fifteen pages are optimal, although up to twenty pages is acceptable for most classes. Also, select material that has fairly broad appeal. Dense theological works or esoteric mystical pieces will rarely capture the attention of class attendees. In planning the meeting all the materials should be described for the attendees and their preferences solicited. If necessary, a ballot can be used, but whenever possible try to reach a consensus. If two sources seem equally attractive or there is a split opinion over two sources, both can be selected by extending out the calendar several weeks. Most topics will run from six to twelve weeks, although shorter sessions can be used for filler. As soon as the selections are made, inform the class at its next meeting what has been selected and ask if there are any objections. Typically, there will be none.

3. Solicit Class Facilitators: An objective of an adult class is to develop leadership. Rotating the class facilitation responsibilities will accomplish this. Not everyone feels comfortable facilitating the class, and that's fine. A group of four to seven facilitators will work just fine. This group will tend to overlap with the planning group and may consist of all the same people. As with the planning group, invite all class members who wish to participate to become a facilitator.

4. Develop a Calendar: Prior to leading a planning meeting the class organizer should have a blank calendar covering the period for planning. Special dates should be identified, for example, holidays and special liturgical seasons such as Advent and Lent. When selecting material one should judge how it will fit into the calendar. Also, decisions need to be reached regarding whether or not to meet on holidays. If a large number of people leave town for the holidays you might arrange for a social time where those in town come and bring some snacks and just socialize during the scheduled class period. Another decision to make is if you desire special studies, especially appropriate for Advent and Lent. Many groups take the summer off, usually tying their schedule to the local school year. We decided a few years ago to go throughout the year and that has worked as well.

5. Schedule Facilitators: Once the material has been selected and ordered, the class organizer will need to assign facilitation dates to the facilitators. I have found email to be the most effective way to do this. Typically, I will make a draft schedule for the facilitators, email it to them, and ask them to respond within a few days regarding their availability on the dates assigned. If a person is not available when assigned then I work around their availability. I try to schedule folks for two consecutive weeks. As the class organizer, I usually take the first two weeks and often reserve the last week for a wrap-up session, which I also lead.

Social Time, Joys, and Concerns

At its best, the class should also function as a support group. That means setting aside some class time for sharing and making a special effort to pay attention to what is going on in class members' lives, both joys and concerns. One or two people can ensure that cards are sent in cases of illness or other absences. For individuals facing difficult circumstances a laying-on of hands with prayer is often deeply appreciated and heartfelt. Also, once or twice annually a class pot luck gathering either at church or if possible at someone's home is an effective bonding tool for the class.

Class Behavior

Class members need to abide by certain behaviors. Here are some basics:

1. Everyone is encouraged to express themselves, but do not have to feel compelled to do so.

2. All comments must be openly respected no matter how radical it may seem at the time.

3. The Facilitator:

    a. May begin and end the class with prayer.

    b. Prepares material and/or questions to kick off the class, but does not dominate the discussion.

    c. Pays attention to the participants and ensures all those with a comment are given time to express it.

    d. Ensures that no one person dominates discussion.

    e. Asks for clarification when something is unclear.

    f. Manages the discussion if it becomes emotional and deals with the emotions before continuing.

4. Class Members:

    a. Agree to respect other's opinions and statements.

    b. Prepare for the class by reviewing the study material as appropriate ahead of the class.

    c. Avoid making bold, inflexible, and uncompromising statements.

    d. Maintain regular attendance.

    e. Participate as appropriate and able in class planning and facilitation.

Good luck and best wishes for a successful adult study group!

Lesson Plans

This section provides session plans that class facilitators may use as a guide for leading discussion. Each session, beginning with the book's preface and for each subsequent section contains a check-in time, a brief introduction, an opening prayer, several examples of questions to stimulate discussion, and a closing prayer. These, of course, are just suggestions to get the class off to a start. Experienced facilitators will either deviate from this format or design a completely different one representing their own particular desires and style.

The check-in time allows the class to slowly come together by sharing some of their experiences of the past week. During this time the facilitator should take note of any particular joys, sorrows, or need for follow-up inquiries during the next week.

The introduction helps people begin to focus on the topic at hand. It should be short, concise, and not be an overall summary of the chapter. The end of the introduction should lead into the opening prayer. Class members' joys or concerns may be included in the opening prayer.

The questions are offered as vehicles for starting the discussion. They may be altered to fit the specific situation or concerns of the class. The discussion period should end about five minutes before the end of the class time. The facilitator may wish to ask for any closing comments or make observations about the discussion as a wrap up. This is not necessary, however. All views should be welcome and no one should be permitted to dominate the discussion. The facilitator should look for opportunities to engage people who may be reticent to talk, but seem to want to say something. This can be determined by looking at body language and facial expressions.

The closing time may contain a closing prayer. A suggested one is provided in the session plan. However, it is perfectly acceptable to ask someone in the group to offer a prayer, and then if no one volunteers the facilitator can do it. This is also a time when reminders can be made about keeping certain issues or concerns in the members' thoughts and prayers during the week. In some cases it may be appropriate for a laying-on of hands for a grieving or saddened member accompanied by an impromptu prayer. After closing there will generally be some visiting before members leave the class.

Preface

Check In

Five to ten minutes for checking in with class members' concerns.

Introduce Topic

In the author's preface the author recognizes the declining membership of Christian churches and the growing number of Americans who declare themselves as unaffiliated with any Christian denomination. He poses the question that the church may be a relic of the past since many of the functions provided by churches have been taken over by governments and other secular groups. He talks about how everyday experience is often incompatible with many orthodox Christian beliefs. He also says that he wrote this book for those desiring a deeper, more intellectually satisfying understanding of Christianity.

Opening Prayer

Gracious Spirit as we begin this new study, we pray that we will be open to its message and how you speak to us today. While we may find criticism with the church, we take it as constructive criticism that we will not respond to defensively, but as an opportunity to undergird our faith in a way that will build upon the revelations of the centuries such that we may draw closer to you. Amen.

Sample Discussion Questions

1. What is your view of the declining church membership?

2. Do you believe the church has a future or is it a relic of the past?

3. What has been your experience with adult study groups? Have they been fulfilling and meaningful? Or have they been too simplistic and perhaps even insulting?

4. Who have been your mentors in faith, perhaps pastors or laypersons?

5. What do you hope to get out of this study?

Closing Prayer

Gentle, compassionate Spirit, within us and among us, help us discern truth such that our faith may be built upon a rock and not the shifting sands of misinformation, charlatanism, ignorance, and personal preference. Let your presence within us inform us with everlasting truth. Amen.

Being Christian

Check In

Five to ten minutes for checking in with class members' concerns.

Introduce Topic

In chapter 1 the idea is presented that what being Christian in the twenty-first century means to many people may need to change. Also, it is indicated that Christianity may need to be understood as having a greater range of freedom in accepting and rejecting certain traditional church doctrines and traditions. A brief sketch is provided for each chapter.

Opening Prayer

Gracious Spirit we come to you understanding that faith, hope, and love abide, but that the greatest of these is love. Being both emotional and rational beings, as we have been created, we open ourselves to a fuller, more robust understanding of faith in this study, a faith, we pray, that will lead to the everlasting presence of Jesus among us. Amen.

Sample Discussion Questions

1. The author believes that declining church membership is in part due to the persistence of archaic expressions of the Christian faith. What do you think he means by this? Do you agree or disagree?

2. Is the author correct in assuming that certain church doctrines may have become obsolete?

3. Are there some teachings you received earlier in your Christian journey to which you no longer subscribe?

4. What is your understanding of what faith is? Is it only a system of beliefs?

5. Does Küng's observation that faith is simultaneously an act of knowing, feeling, and willing make sense to you?

6. Do you agree with the author's distinction between knowing and believing? Why or why not?

7. The author speaks about a tension between how the world is and how it could or should be. How have you felt this tension? How does one's faith play a role in how this tension plays out?

8. It is said the Gospel means Good News. What do you think the good news of the Gospel really is?

Closing Prayer

Gentle, compassionate Spirit, help us discern truth such that our faith may be strengthened and deepened throughout this study. Be present with us as we explore in-depth the topics in the chapters that follow. Amen.

2

Justification by Faith

Check In

Five to ten minutes for checking in with class members' concerns.

Introduce Topic

Chapter 2 begins with a discussion of how "justified by faith" has been used as a proof text to divide people over the centuries, opposed to Paul's unifying intention. It is followed by a discussion of the controversies found in Paul's writings in the mid-first century. A distinction is made between what we know are Paul's writings and what has been called the pseudo-Pauline letters. It is noted that unlike Jesus who ministered mostly in the more remote villages and countryside of Galilee, Paul took his message right to the major urban centers of the Roman Empire. The chapter describes some of the upheaval that existed at the time and the migration of people into these areas. Paul worked for the tearing down of barriers that existed in the highly stratified Roman society. He argued that we are all one in Christ Jesus and when we internalized this we would act out of this oneness and be justified with God. Let us begin with prayer.

Opening Prayer

Good and Gracious One, our greatest and most ardent act of worship is to emulate your goodness in our everyday living. We pray that as we continue our faithful journey we will know that it is not our will that dominates;

rather, as it was with Paul, it is the Christ Spirit living in us. And that being the case, we will struggle to tear down the barriers that separate us and embrace in love all of your children. Amen.

Sample Discussion Questions

1. Why is Paul sometimes misunderstood?

2. Have you ever thought about how cultural norms have influenced Scripture?

3. How did the conditions of the time make Paul's work to create Christian communities attractive?

4. Who were the God Fearers? What attracted these people to the synagogues? Why were these people obvious targets for Paul's evangelism?

5. Why did some Jews attack Paul when he entered synagogues in the cities of the empire?

6. Why was "there is neither Jew not Greek, neither slave nor free, nor is there male and female, for you are all one in Christ Jesus" so radical a statement for Paul to make?

7. What do you think Paul mean by "justified by faith"? How has this over the centuries separated people rather than united them?

8. What are some of the social barriers Christians have that separate God's children? Would Paul, if he were teaching today, encourage us to tear these down? How might this be done?

Closing Prayer

Spirit of Truth and Compassion, help us to open ourselves to you and to love all your children. When our actions work toward this we can be assured that we are truly justified in your presence. Amen.

3

Jesus: The Fully Human One

Check In

Five to ten minutes for checking in with class members' concerns.

Introduce Topic

Chapter 3 begins by making a distinction between Jesus of Nazareth and the post-Easter Christ. There is a brief discussion of the various titles assigned to Jesus after his crucifixion and resurrection to express who people thought he was. Many of the titles had been previously used in the Hebrew Scriptures or had been reserved for Caesar. Appendices I and II contain background for this chapter and may be referred to for a more in-depth historical or contextual description of first-century Galilee. The chapter integrates late scholarship from archaeological studies as well as sociological analysis to provide a more sophisticated analysis than has previously been available. From this perspective, Jesus's ministry is then put into the matrix of his time, focusing on historical, political, economic, health, and religious dimensions. In it Jesus is depicted as being the fully human one into which humanity may someday evolve. But before we begin, let us pray.

Opening Prayer

Generous Spirit, one who incarnated Jesus with your full human dimension, we pray that the time may become short when all your human creation eschews their inhumanity and become fully human as was Jesus, our model and truly our savior. Amen.

Sample Discussion Questions

1. Has it ever bothered you that we so frequently use the term Jesus Christ as though it was a first name and last name?

2. Do you agree with the author that Jesus may have come out of a middle class family, perhaps as a master builder?

3. Do you think that Jesus received his knowledge of Scripture though divine revelation or though schooling as our author suggests?

4. Was Jesus political? Why or why not?

5. Jesus spent almost all his ministry in Galilee. Why do you think he did this?

6. What evidence is there that Galilee was predominantly Jewish in the first century CE?

7. How would you describe the economy of first-century Galilee?

8. Why do you think there are so many cases of Jesus's healing in the Gospels? What is the significance of this?

9. What was the teaching of the elders and why do you think Jesus objected to it?

10. Did Jesus come to start a new religion apart from Judaism? What was his goal?

11. Was Jesus a fool and failure or a mystic visionary or neither?

Closing Prayer

Spirit of Compassion, help us to open ourselves to you and see the inhumanity that still dwells within us. Help us cast this aside and work to internalize all those values that you incarnated in Jesus. Help us, one and all, evolve into that fully human being you ultimately intend for us and illustrated through the life and teachings of Jesus. Amen.

4

From Criminal to Christ

Check In

Five to ten minutes for checking in with class members' concerns.

Introduce Topic

In chapter 4 we address Christ, how Jesus went from being a prophet and teacher to the Messiah or in Greek, the Christ. The horror of crucifixion is described, and Howard Thurman's point about Christ as object rather than subject is explored. We look at Christian doctrine and ask if some of it needs to be discarded. Let us begin with prayer.

Opening Prayer

Gentle eternal Spirit, living Christ, subject of our devotion, inspiration of our worship, help us to understand you in ways our knowledge and culture can understand. Let us keep you in the center of our lives and avoid making you an object that we use or fear rather than emulate. Amen.

Sample Discussion Questions

1. What is the difference between the pre-Easter Jesus and the post Easter Christ?

2. How would you explain Howard Thurman's idea of treating Christ as an object vs. a subject?

3. Is Christ treated as a subject or an object in our postmodern culture?

4. What do you think is the meaning of the doubting Thomas episode in the Gospel of John? Is this to be taken literally or metaphorically?

5. Can a story be true, but not literally true?

6. Is there bathwater that should be discarded in Christianity?

7. What do you think the author was alluding to regarding Jesus being fully human?

8. Can you describe a time when you were awakened to the spirit of the divine, a time when you had a mystical moment?

Closing Prayer

Loving and eternal Christ, open us to your presence within us, like you were within Paul when he said, "It is not I, but Christ living in me." We seek to awaken to your spirit, help us to make room for you to make this happen. Amen.

5

Atonement

Check In

Five to ten minutes for checking in with class members' concerns.

Introduce Topic

In chapter 5 we address the question of atonement. What is it, what are its roots in the Old Testament, how was it expressed in the New Testament, what forms did it take over the centuries, and what are some of its underlying assumptions. A twenty-first-century concept of atonement is advanced at the chapter's end. Let us begin with prayer.

Opening Prayer

Beloved Spirit, you are shrouded in a mystery we will never fully understand. We are grateful for the example of Jesus and we ask for the strength and courage to grow more fully like him each day and becoming more fully of the nature you have planned for us. Amen.

Sample Discussion Questions

1. What has been your impression of Old Testament cultic sacrifice?

2. How would you describe the god these practices were instituted for?

3. Can you wrap your mind around blood being a spiritual detergent?

4. What do you think of the author's assertion that Paul wrote metaphorically about Jesus's death being a cultic sacrifice?

5. What is your impression of the atonement explanations over the centuries? How has the culture and state of understanding of the day influenced them?

6. Why do you think twenty-first-century Christians still cling to cultic sacrificial atonement theology?

7. How have the Old Testament prophets influence been counter to the cultic practice of their day.

8. Do you find substitutionary atonement to be a satisfying grounding for your faith?

9. What is your impression of humanity in a state of evolution as proposed by Irenaeus, Chardin, and Spong?

10. Do you have an understanding of how atonement is achieved that differs from substitutionary atonement? From the author's understanding of atonement?

Closing Prayer

We all wish to live according to your will, Great Spirit. We are grateful for the example of Jesus whom we pray we can grow to be more like. Give us the strength and courage to do this. Amen.

6

Is Jesus the Only Way?

Check In

Five to ten minutes for checking in with class members' concerns.

Introduce Topic

In chapter 6 we address the question, "Is Jesus the only path to the divine?" The historical development of the Gospel of John and how it differs from the Synoptic Gospels is discussed. John's extensive use of metaphor is developed as an indication of how this Gospel should be read. John's preoccupation with the Jews is put into context. Let us begin with prayer.

Opening Prayer

Beloved Spirit, we know that religious fervor has been the source of much joy, but also the driver for interreligious intolerance and inhumane action. We seek a deeper understanding of the motivations and context in which the ancient Scriptures were written so that we may put them in perspective. We need a broader understanding of salvation and how it relates to our everyday lives. We pray that we can continue our journey to a fuller and more mature faith learning from all sources of divine experience. Amen.

Sample Discussion Questions

1. How have you understood John 14:6, "No one comes to the Father except through me," up until now?

2. Has this chapter given you a new understanding as to why the author(s) of John may have written this Gospel as they did?

3. How do the author(s) of John poke fun at literal interpretation?

4. Are there examples where you see exaggeration or embellishment in the Gospel of John?

5. Why do you think John makes such use of metaphor?

6. Can you give examples of other parts of the Bible that make use of metaphor?

7. Why did the Gentile Christians take most of the heat during the various Roman persecutions of Christians?

8. Why do you think the authors of John made such an issue with the Jews in the Gospel story?

9. Was Jesus starting a new religion or reforming Judaism? If reforming, how was he doing this?

10. Can other world religions inform us about the nature of God?

Closing Prayer

The crucifixion of Jesus and the destruction left both the early Christian and Jewish communities in a state of confusion. We understand that the controversies of early Christianity were controversies within the Jewish community. We pray that our future controversies and discussions between religions will be held with mutual understanding and good will within the kingdom of your children. Let there be peace on earth and good will toward all. Amen.

7

Scripture: Word of God or Word of Man?

Check In

Five to ten minutes for checking in with class members' concerns.

Introduce Topic

In chapter 7 Scripture is addressed. What is it, what authority does it have, how we should read it. How did our ideas about God develop and why there seems to be so many conflicting aspects the God's character are discussed. The impact of culture creep and how it waters down Scripture is also discussed. Let us begin with prayer.

Opening Prayer

Generous Spirit that has inspired and touched so many of your children over the centuries, we pray that their experiences of you, whether cast in poetry, prose, or metaphor, may inspire and inform us. We pray that we discern the radical challenges expressed in Scripture from those parts that have been watered down by cultural influences. We pray that you help us discern your truth in Scripture apart from sections altered to be more culturally acceptable. Amen.

Sample Discussion Questions

1. Is it appropriate to follow a reading of Scripture with the words, "The word of God for the people of God"? Why or why not? How might this be rephrased?

2. How does our educational system condition us to read literally instead of critically?

3. What are your thoughts regarding Dever's conclusion that the bloody genocides of Numbers, Joshua, and elsewhere never happened?

4. Have you ever thought of the Bible as containing humor?

5. What has been your way of reconciling the vengeful God with the compassionate God?

6. How do the ideas of Borg, Crossan, and Rohr about the Bible accommodating culture help explain contradictions in Scripture?

7. If the Scriptures are not the literal word of God, how are we to read them, and are they therefore less sacred or authoritative for us in the twenty-first century?

8. Are there Scriptures that can't be taken literally? That can be? What might they be?

9. How then should we read and use Scripture?

Closing Prayer

We not only pray for the insight to better understand Scripture, but also the tenacity to engage in continuing religious education so that we might develop an ever-more mature Christian faith. Amen.

8

God

Check In

Five to ten minutes for checking in with class members' concerns.

Introduce Topic

In chapter 8 we are going to address the meaning of God. Can we think of God as other than a super being that comes to our rescue at times, but other times doesn't? Is God something we dust off and use when we reach the end of our own resources? Where can we find God? What does it mean for God to be the "great beyond in or midst" or the "ground of all being and all becoming"? These and other topics are in this chapter. Let us begin with prayer.

Opening Prayer

Divine presence, may we ever-more fully come to sense you and draw nearer to your vision for humanity. Help us, not only see your presence in us, but also in all with whom we encounter. We pray that our petty irritations and self-seeking supremacy might be overcome by the inspiration of your love for us and our realization that our loving you means we must love all within whom you dwell. Amen.

Sample Discussion Questions

1. What do you think Bonhoeffer meant by thinking of God as the "great beyond in our midst"?

2. In what ways can you conceive of God as not a being, but the "ground of being and all becoming"?

3. Can we think of God other than in anthropomorphic (i.e. human like) terms?

4. How can an apophatic (i.e., a negation) approach help us gain a better understanding of God?

5. Why should we not think of miracles as supernatural events?

6. Can you describe some very common events that are indeed miracles?

7. Where is God?

8. How does the idea that God lies in the depths of each one of us change the dynamic of individualism? What might be the significance of this?

9. What might it mean that we haven't evolved into being fully human?

Closing Prayer

Good and gracious spirit, we pray as we leave this gathering that we grow in our knowledge of you. That we continue to learn more about what you are not as well as what you wish for us to embody and emulate. We pray for the sensitivity to experience your unifying spiritual energy and draw nearer to all we encounter. We pray that we become sensitive to the awe and wonder of the miracles of normalcy. We pray that we find our true self in which you reside and in that revelation become your loving sons and daughters. Amen.

9

Church

Check In

Five to ten minutes for checking in with class members' concerns.

Introduce Topic

In chapter 9 we are going to address the church, particularly its need for reform and its role in the twenty-first century. Let us begin with prayer.

Opening Prayer

Spirit of truth and beauty, revealed deep within us when we make the room, touch us today and imbue us with wisdom as we seek to find ways to make your church ever more responsive to your vision for creation. Amen.

Sample Discussion Questions

1. Why do you think the fastest growing segment of our population is unaffiliated church members?

2. Did Jesus die for your sins? Why or why not? How might this be rephrased for the twenty-first century?

3. How does evolution change the way we have understood Jesus and his role in salvation?

4. Would deemphasizing sinfulness, but emphasizing empowerment to become more like Jesus be a better Christian message? Why or why not?

5. In what ways might the church be too acculturated or nationalistic?

6. Do you agree with Kaufman's commandments to act, act morally, and act ethically?

7. Is there a case for the church not to act morally? What would it be?

8. How can clergy be more up front about the Christianity they studied in seminary?

9. Should parishioners be obligated to better educate themselves in a mature theology? How can this happen?

10. In what ways should the church be more involved in politics?

11. What ideas do you have that will strengthen the church in the current age?

12. Do you think it is time for the church to reinvent itself?

13. How can we best experience the living Christ?

Closing Prayer

Spirit, deep within each of us, we pray that we might find the courage, wisdom, and insight to live the ideals we discussed today, and that we may be the change that we desire to see come to fruition. Amen.

Epilogue

Check In

Five to ten minutes for checking in with class members' concerns.

Introduce Topic

The topics in this book have been exhausted. It is now time to critique the experience. Let us begin with prayer.

Opening Prayer

Dear God, we pray that our minds be open and our hearts warmed as today we complete this study. May we feel your presence as we open ourselves to the meaning of your being in our lives. Amen.

Sample Discussion Questions

1. What is your overall impression of this book?

2. What parts of the book did you find particularly difficult to accept? What parts brought new insight to you?

3. What do you think needs to be done to reverse the decline in Christianity?

4. Is it still necessary to have the church in postmodern society? Why or why not?

5. Is spirituality dead or just being nurtured in places other than the church?

6. How can your church become more vital in your community?

Closing Prayer

Good and gracious God, we turn to you in gratitude for the time we have been together studying and discussing this book. We pray that our faith journey not end here but that we continue to grow in our understanding and appreciation of you and your creation. Amen.

Bibliography

Adams, Samuel L. *Social and Economic Life in Second Temple Judea*. Louisville: Westminster John Knox, 2014.

"America's Changing Religious Landscape." Pew Research Center, May 12, 2015. http://www.pewforum.org/2015/05/12/americas-changing-religious-landscape/.

Anderson, Paul N. *The Fourth Gospel and the Quest for Jesus: Modern Foundations Reconsidered*. London: T & T Clark, 2006.

———. *The Riddles of the Fourth Gospel: An Introduction to John*. Minneapolis: Fortress, 2011.

Aviam, Mordechai. "People, Land, Economy, and Belief in First-Century Galilee and its Origins: A Comparative Archaeological Synthesis." In *The Galilean Economy in the Time of Jesus*, edited by David A. Fiensy and Ralph K. Hawkins, 5–48. Atlanta: Society of Biblical Literature, 2013.

———. "Socio-economical Hierarchy and its Economical Foundations in First Century Galilee: The Evidence from Yodefat and Gamla." In *Flavius Josephus: Interpretation and History*, edited by Jack Pastor et al., 29–38. Leiden: Brill, 2011.

Berlin, Andrea M. "Manifest Identity: From Ioudaios to Jew." In *Between Cooperation and Hostility: Multiple Identities in Ancient Judaism and the Interaction with Foreign Powers*, edited by Rainer Albertz and Jakob Wöhrle, 151–75. Göttingen, Germany: Vandenhoeck and Ruprecht, 2013.

Bonhoeffer, Dietrich. *Letters and Papers from Prison*. Edited by Eberhard Bethge. New York: Touchstone, 1997.

Borg, Marcus J. *Speaking Christian: Why Christian Words have Lost Their Meaning and Power and How They can Be Restored*. New York: HarperOne, 2011.

Borg, Marcus J., and John Dominic Crossan. *The First Paul: Reclaiming the Radical Visionary Behind the Church's Conservative Icon*. New York: HarperOne, 2009.

———. *The Last Week: What the Gospels Really Teach about Jesus's Final Days in Jerusalem*. New York: HarperCollins, 2006.

Boyarin, Daniel. *The Jewish Gospels: The Story of the Jewish Christ*. New York: New Press, 2012. Kindle edition.

Brown, Raymond E. *The Community of the Beloved Disciple: The Life, Loves, and Hates of an Individual Church in New Testament Times*. New York: Paulist, 1979.

Brueggemann, Walter. *Chosen? Reading the Bible Amid the Israeli-Palestinian Conflict.* Louisville: Westminster John Knox, 2015.

Charlesworth, James H., and Mordechai Aviam. "Reconstructing First-Century Galilee: Reflections on Ten Major Problems." In *Jesus Research: New Methodologies and Perceptions,* edited by James H. Charlesworth, 103–37. Grand Rapids: Eerdmans, 2014.

Choi, Agnes. "Never the Two Shall Meet? Urban-Rural Interaction in Lower Galilee." In *Galilee in the Second Temple and Mishnaic Periods.* Vol. 1, *Life, Culture, and Society,* edited by David A. Fiensy and James Riley Strange, 297–311. Minneapolis: Fortress, 2014.

Cobb, John B., and David Ray Griffin. *Process Theology: An Introductory Exposition.* Louisville: Westminster John Knox, 1976.

Cox, Harvey. *The Future of Faith.* New York: HarperOne, 2009.

Crossan, John Dominic. *Jesus: A Revolutionary Biography.* San Francisco: HarperCollins, 1994.

Crossan, John Dominic, and Jonathan L. Reed. *Excavating Jesus: Beneath the Stones, Behind the Texts.* New York: HarperCollins, 2001.

Deines, Roland. "The Pharisees between 'Judaisms' and 'Common Judaisms.'" In *Justification and Varigated Nomism.* Vol. 1, *The Complexities of Second Temple Judaism,* edited by D. A. Carson et al., 443–504. Tubingen, Germany: Mohr Siebeck, 2001.

Dever, William G. *What Did the Biblical Writers Know and When Did They Know It? What Archaeology can Tell Us about the Reality of Ancient Israel.* Grand Rapids: Eerdmans, 2001.

———. *Who Were the Early Israelites and Where Did They Come From.* Grand Rapids: Eerdmans, 2003.

Eliav, Yaron Z. "Jews and Judaism 70–429 CE." In *A Companion to the Roman Empire,* edited by David S. Potter, 565–86. Malden, MA: Blackwell, 2006.

Farrer, Austin. "Revelation." In *Faith and Logic: Oxford Essays in Philosophical Religion,* edited by Basil Mitchell, 84–107. New York: Routledge, 2013.

Fiensy, David A. "Assessing the Economy of Galilee in the Late Second Temple Period: Five Considerations." In *The Galilean Economy in the Time of Jesus,* edited by David A. Fiensy and Ralph K. Hawkins, 165–86. Atlanta: Society of Biblical Literature, 2013.

———. "The Galilean Village in the Late Second Temple and Mishnaic Periods." In *Galilee in the Late Second Temple and Mishnaic Periods.* Vol. 1, *Life, Culture, and Society,* edited by David A. Fiensy and James Riley Strange, 177–207. Minneapolis: Fortress, 2014.

Finlan, Stephen. *Problems with Atonement.* Collegeville, MN: Liturgical, 2005.

France, R. T. *The Gospel of Matthew.* The New International Commentary on the New Testament. Grand Rapids: Eerdmans, 2007.

Fredriksen, Paula. "Christians in the Roman Empire." In *A Companion to the Roman Empire,* edited by David S. Potter, 587–606. Malden, MA: Blackwell, 2006.

Funk, Robert W., et al. *The Five Gospels: What Did Jesus Really Say? The Search for the Authentic Words of Jesus.* New York: Macmillan, 1993.

Gal, Zvi. *Lower Galilee During the Iron Age.* Translated by Marcia Reines Josephy. American Schools of Oriental Research Dissertation Series 8. Winona Lake, IN: Eisenbrauns, 1992.

Hahn, Thich Nhat. *Peace of Mind: Becoming Fully Present*. Berkeley: Parallax, 2013.

Hengel, Martin. *Crucifixion in the Ancient World and the Folly of the Message of the Cross*. Philadelphia: Fortress, 1977. Kindle edition.

Hiebert, Theodore. *The Yahwist's Landscape: Nature and Religion in Early Israel*. New York: Oxford University Press, 1996.

Horsley, Richard A., and John S. Hanson. *Bandits, Prophets, and Messiahs: Popular Movements at the Time of Jesus*. New York: HarperCollins, 1985.

van Houwelingen, P. H. R. "Fleeing Forward: The Departure of Christians from Jerusalem to Pella." *Westminster Theological Journal* 65 (2003) 181–200.

Johnson, Paul. *A History of Christianity*. New York: Atheneum, 1977.

Kaufman, Gordon D. *In Face of Mystery: A Constructive Theology*. Cambridge: Harvard University Press, 1993.

Klink, Edward W. "Expulsion from the Synagogue?: Rethinking a Johannine Anachronism." *Tyndale Bulletin* 59 (2008) 99–118.

Knitter, Paul F. *Without Buddha I Could Not Be a Christian*. Oxford: One World, 2009.

Korb, Scott. *Life in Year One: What the World was Like in First-Century Palestine*. New York: Riverhead, 2010.

Küng, Hans. *On Being a Christian*. Translated by Edward Quinn. Garden City, NY: Image, 1984.

Kushner, Harold S. *When Bad Things Happen to Good People*. New York: Avon, 1981.

Marney, Carlyle. *Priests to Each Other*. Valley Forge, PA: Judson, 1974.

Mattila, Sharon L. "Inner Life in Galilee: A Diverse and Complex Phenomenon." In *Galilee in the Second Temple and Mishnaic Periods*. Vol. 1, *Life, Culture, and Society*, edited by David A. Fiensy and James Riley Strange, 312–45. Minneapolis: Fortress, 2014.

Mattingly, David. "The Imperial Economy." In *A Companion to the Roman Empire*, edited by David S. Potter, 283–97. Malden, MA: Blackwell, 2006.

McLaren, Brian. *The Great Spiritual Migration: How the World's Largest Religion is Seeking a Better Way to Be Christian*. New York: Convergent, 2016.

Meyers, Robin. *Saving Jesus from the Church: How to Stop Worshiping Christ and Start Following Jesus*. New York: HarperCollins, 2009.

———. *The Underground Church: Reclaiming the Subversive Way of Jesus*. San Francisco: Jossey-Bass, 2012.

Neihardt, John G. *Black Elk Speaks*. Albany: State University of New York Press, 2008.

Newell, John Philip. *The Rebirthing of God: Christianity's Struggle for New Beginnings*. Woodstock, VT: SkyLight Paths, 2014.

Niebuhr, Reinhold. *An Interpretation of Christian Ethics*. New York: HarperOne, 1987.

Outler, Albert C., ed. *John Wesley*. Oxford: Oxford University Press, 1964.

Poirier, John C. "Education/Literacy in Jewish Galilee: Was There Any and at What Level?" In *Galilee in the Second Temple and Mishnaic Periods*. Vol. 1, *Life, Culture, and Society*, edited by David A. Fiensy and James Riley Strange, 253–60. Minneapolis: Fortress, 2014.

Rasmussen, Larry L. *Earth-Honoring Faith: Religious Ethics in a New Key*. New York: Oxford University Press, 2013.

Reed, Jonathan L. *Archaeology and the Galilean Jesus: A Re-examination of the Evidence*. Harrisburg: Trinity, 2000.

———. "Mortality, Morbidity, and Economics in Jesus' Galilee." In *Galilee in the Second Temple and Mishnaic Periods*. Vol. 1, *Life, Culture, and Society*, edited by David A. Fiensy and James Riley Strange, 242–52. Minneapolis: Fortress, 2014.

Rohr, Richard. *Dancing Standing Still: Healing the World from a Place of Prayer*. New York: Paulist, 2014. Kindle edition.

———. *Things Hidden: Scripture as Spirituality*. Cincinnati: St. Anthony Messenger, 2014.

Seneca, Lucius Annaeus. *Letters from a Stoic*. Translated by Robin Campbell. London: Penguin, 1969.

Schillebeeckx, Edward. *The Understanding of Faith: Interpretation and Criticism*. New York: Seabury, 1974.

Schüssler Fiorenza, Elizabeth. *In Memory of Her: A Feminist Theological Reconstruction of Christian Origins*. New York: Crossroad, 1987.

Shanks, Hershel, et al. *The Rise of Ancient Israel*. Washington, DC: Biblical Archaeology Society, 2012.

Smith, Mark. *The Early History of God: Yahweh and the Other Deities in Ancient Israel*. 2nd ed. Grand Rapids: Eerdmans, 2002.

Spong, John Shelby. *Biblical Literalism: A Gentile Heresy*. New York: HarperOne, 2016.

———. *The Fourth Gospel: Tales of a Jewish Mystic*. New York: HarperOne, 2013.

———. *Jesus for the Non-Religious*. New York: HarperOne, 2007.

Stark, Rodney. *The Rise of Christianity: How the Obscure, Marginal Jesus Movement became the Dominant Religious Force in the Western World in a Few Centuries*. Princeton: Princeton University Press, 1996.

———. *The Triumph of Christianity: How the Jesus Movement became the World's Largest Religion*. New York: HarperOne, 2011.

Teilhard de Chardin, Pierre. *Christianity and Evolution*. Translated by René Hague. London: Harcourt Brace Jovanovich, 1971.

Thurman, Howard. *Jesus and the Disinherited*. Nashville: Abingdon, 1949.

Tillich, Paul. *The Shaking of the Foundations*. New York: Scribner, 1948.

Udoh, Fabian. "Taxation and Other Sources of Government Income in the Galilee of Herod and Antipas." In *Galilee in the Second Temple and Mishnaic Periods*. Vol. 1, *Life, Culture, and Society*, edited by David A. Fiensy and James Riley Strange, 366–87. Minneapolis: Fortress, 2014.

United Methodist Church. *The United Methodist Hymnal*. Nashville: Abingdon, 1989.

Vosper, Gretta. *With or Without God: Why the Way We Live is More Important than What We Believe*. Toronto: Harper Perennial, 2008.

Weaver, J. Denny. "Violence in Christian Theology." *Cross Currents* 51 (2001) 150–76. http://www.crosscurrents.org/weaver0701.htm.

Wink, Walter. *The Human Being: Jesus and the Enigma of the Son of the Man*. Minneapolis: Fortress, 2002.

———. *The Powers that Be: Theology for a New Millennium*. New York: Doubleday, 1998.

Yoder, John Howard. *The Original Revolution*. Scottsdale, PA: Herald, 1971.